The sociology of secularisation

International Library of Sociology

Founded by Karl Mannheim

Editor: John Rex, University of Warwick

Arbor Scientiae
Arbor Vitae

A catalogue of the books available in the **International Library of Sociology** and other series of Social Science books published by Routledge & Kegan Paul will be found at the end of this volume.

The sociology of secularisation

A critique of a concept

Peter E. Glasner

Department of Sociology
Australian National University

Routledge & Kegan Paul

London, Henley and Boston

First published in 1977
by Routledge & Kegan Paul Ltd
39 Store Street,
London WC1E 7DD,
Broadway House,
Newtown Road,
Henley-on-Thames,
Oxon RG9 1EN and
9 Park Street,
Boston, Mass. 02108, USA
Set in 10 on 11 pt Times Linotype
and printed in Great Britain by
Willmer Brothers Limited, Birkenhead

ISBN 0 7100 8455 2

Contents

CONTENTS

Preface

This book is an exercise in the methodology of sociology. It is concerned with the relationships that exist between theory and research, and has as its focus the concept of secularisation. By grounding this concept in definitions of religion, it illuminates the theoretical paucity of a sociological sub-discipline once the central concern of the Founding Fathers. The main brunt of the argument is that no scientific theory of the secularisation process has been developed; and research done has, at best, provided an example of *systematic empiricism*. This part of the book utilises the notion of sociological myth to provide evidence for such a contention.

Following the analysis of the criteria by which sociological myths may be recognised, the first section is concerned with the substantive evidence behind the assertion that secularisation has attained mythical status. The various processes subsumed under its general headings are classified into three categories according to the definitions of religion which form their bases. At least one process from each category is explored in detail.

The discussion then moves in the second section to why the substantive analyses cannot be generalised in any theoretical manner but remain empirically rooted. In this way the underlying rationale for the development of the major secularisation processes in sociology is exposed as stemming from the, often implicit, values of contemporary Western sociologists. The secularisation processes are recognised as part of a more general ideology of progress which distorts or misuses analyses, located in specific co-ordinates of time and space, and by doing so attempts to provide generalisations from empirical rather than theoretical roots.

Finally, there is an attempt to produce an adequate theory of religion and the religious, which not only illuminates the empiricist nature of the previous analyses, but also allocates a more clearly defined role to the concept of secularisation. In doing so it reveals the generic function of the term, and its utility in social engineering. In this way, the discussion returns to the concept of sociological myth and its intervention as a gloss on the disjunction between systematic empiricism and theoretical practice.

I would like to acknowledge the Social Science Research Council, whose grant funded the University of London doctoral thesis upon which this book is based. I would also like to thank the Department of Sociology at the Australian National University for support both in time and resources. My intellectual debts are more difficult to enumerate, but I would particularly like to mention Dr I. M. Edwards, M. J. Rustin, D. Young, Professor D. A. Martin, and A. Hale Glasner. Finally I owe a huge debt of thanks to the typists: Zeta Hall and Ettie Oakman.

Parts of chapter 3 have appeared as: ' "Idealisation" and the Social Myth of Secularisation', in M. Hill (ed.), *A Sociological Yearbook of Religion in Britain*, vol. 8, SCM Press, London, 1975, pp. 7–14.

1 Introduction
Social and scientific myths

The notion of myth is a complex one, and open to a variety of interpretations. It is generally accepted that it provides the means by
which communication between individuals in society is facilitated.
It is also accepted that it is a basis by which man can come to
terms with the unknown (Maranda, 1972:12). However, myths go
further than this in that they can also be described as fictitious in
some way. They represent rather than reflect reality. Often this
representation is rooted in a popular idea concerning natural or
historical phenomena.[1]

Frankfort has argued for the existence of 'mythopoeic' thought
which existed in a variety of preliterate and early societies. An
important element in such thought is the inability to trace causal
connections between phenomena, and the concomitantly arbitrary
nature of supposedly causal linkages.

> In every case where we could see no more than association of
> thought, the mythopoeic mind finds a causal connection. Every
> resemblance, every contact in space or time, establishes a
> connection between two objects or events which make it
> possible to see in the one the cause of changes observed in the
> other (Frankfort *et al.*, 1949:27).

He goes on to suggest that an understanding of their relationship stems from an initial conviction that one comes from the
other. Hence, the myths under discussion reflect, in some way, the
prior conceptualisations of the community from which they arise.

Toulmin has argued that contemporary myths stem not from
anthropomorphic interpretations of the natural world, but from
science. He talks of using scientific conceptions to provide a 'tidy,

1

simple and especially an all purpose picture of the world' (Toulmin, 1973 : 68).

Scientific myths can, then, be used to legitimate a broad range of prior value orientations. Barnett, for example, when discussing recent trends in ethology, suggests that much popular writing in the field subscribes to just this kind of scientific myth-making. He says that the most common scientific myths are : 'based on illegitimate inferences based upon the supposed behaviour of animals, or about animals based on the actual behaviour of man' (Barnett, 1973 : 68).

However, as Toulmin points out, it is just because contemporary myths are scientific in origin that they are rarely identified as being myths at all (Toulmin, 1957 : 16). The following discussion, based upon conventional definitions of religion and secularisation, will suggest that a sub-type of the scientific myth in sociology is the *social* myth. It will further be suggested that its presence can be recognised by criteria initially outlined by Toulmin.

Only certain kinds of conceptions are open to the myth-making process. For example, it is difficult to suggest that industrialisation or bureaucratisation are myths. Social scientists have many criteria by which to judge whether or not a society falls into either category. These demarcation criteria are clear, and they are also public. Social myths, on the other hand, are built up with concepts whose demarcation criteria are not explicit. In these grey areas, the basis for distinctions appears to lie within private values. Giddens suggests that while these grey concepts contain elements of truth, they are at the same time distortions of that truth. In discussing four myths that have developed about Durkheim and nineteenth-century sociology he says: 'These interpretations, I want to argue, are "mythological", while they are very widely accepted, they are either false or highly misleading . . .' (Giddens, 1972 : 357).

He then goes on to suggest that it is not wholly accurate to represent Durkheim, and sociology at that stage of its development, as responding to the 'problem of order', or deriving directly from the French and Industrial Revolutions. Nor is it wholly true to characterise the development of social thought in the nineteenth century as reflecting a division between pre-scientific and scientific forms of analysis, while to suggest that since that period it has developed along the dichotomous lines of 'integration' and 'coercion theory' is misleading.

Much of this form of myth-making is based upon that element in mythopoeic thought that isolates a particular relationship between variables to the exclusion of others, and without sound basis for doing so. Thus Armer and Schnaiberg, when analysing the 'near myth' of individual modernity, say:

Underlying most research in this area are premises that a single dimension of modernisation exists along which societies can be distributed, that societies at each point along this continuum tend to share certain social and cultural patterns, and that these socio-cultural patterns lead to, result from, or occur concomitantly with patterns in values, beliefs and behaviours of individuals (Armer and Schnaiberg, 1972:301).

Several writers have expressed similar disquiet about the concepts of 'modernisation' and 'development'. Aron, in discussing under-developed societies, says that according to most studies all they have in common is that they are 'neither modern nor industrialised' (Aron, 1964:30). Bernstein, in objecting to this simplistic and mythical traditional-modern dichotomy, says: 'it should be emphasised that the traditional-modern dichotomy in itself has only a heuristic function, designating an ideal-type destination' (Bernstein, 1971:147).

Dean Tipps has observed that the comparative study of societies, especially with reference to modernisation, needs to be placed within a similarly critical perspective. He feels that received traditions within Western culture play too great a role in its conceptualisation. There appear, in fact, to be a variety of 'modernisation theories', whose areas of agreement are at best superficial (Tipps, 1973:202). Tipps suggest that:

The popularity of the notion of modernisation must be sought not in its clarity and precision as a vehicle of scholarly communication, but rather in its ability to evoke vague and generalised images which serve to summarise all the various transformations of social life attendant upon the rise of industrialisation and the nation state in the late eighteenth and nineteenth centuries (Tipps, 1973: 199).

He concludes that the functions of the concept appear to be primarily ideological and cognitive, serving to 'situate' modern man in his changing social environment. Modernisation may not be a concept at all; it may be an illusion. In this, Tipps echoes Durkheim's critique of Comte, in which he accuses Comte of identifying:

historical development with the idea he had of it, which does not differ much from the layman. Viewed from a distance, history does convey well enough this serial and simple aspect, appearing as a mere succession of individuals proceeding in the

3

same direction because they have the same human nature. Since, moreover, it seems inconceivable to these writers that social evolution could possibly be anything but the development of some human idea, it appears quite natural to define it by the idea men form about it. Now, in proceeding thus, not only does one remain in the sphere of ideology, but one assigns to sociology a concept which is not even truly sociological (Durkheim, 1938:19–20).

The theoretical and spatio-temporal co-ordinates seem to get lost in the myth-making process once the myth has taken hold. It becomes increasingly apparent that original concepts have their meaning extended or altered in accord with the terms of the myth in question. Giddens (1972:358) notes that 'collective elaboration' by subsequent writers is a necessary contributory factor in the mythification process.[2]

Methodological and substantive aspects of myth

Social myths, like their scientific counterparts, have two aspects, which can be labelled:
(a) substantive, relating to the ways in which evidence is collected and used to answer fundamental questions, and
(b) methodological, concerned with whether the methods used for relating the theories and hypotheses to empirical reality are legitimate.

The exploration of the basis of the development of social myth through its methodology facilitates recognition of the substantive aspect.

Methodology is used to legitimate theory by providing an understanding of the means by which empirical validation is possible. The difference between the language used by historians – which is primarily descriptive – and sociologists – which is (or at least should be) primarily propositional (Zetterberg, 1954) – has resulted in the reliance on 'common usage'. The sociologist develops his own technical vocabulary in order to provide a general terminology. The historian, however, is not concerned with abstract approximation but with the 'rich local colour of the language of sources'. The language of sources provides definitions rooted in historical reality and therefore limited by it. The myth of common usage mistakes the language of sources for a technical vocabulary. This problem is ably dealt with by Hindess (1973) in his critique of both positivistic sociology and ethnomethodology. His call, from a different perspective, is also for the need to provide a theoretical problematic divorced from the 'language of sources'.

Whenever the concept of 'common usage' appears in the sociological literature, the most obvious question that springs to mind is
'Whose?' Generally this question can be answered in two ways.
First, it is the 'usage' most commonly found (by statistical or content analysis, for example) within the social structure under investigation. Alternatively it is the 'usage' found among a particular
group (or among several groupings) which are judged important
or significant with reference to the concept under discussion. Objections may be raised concerning the validity of either approach;
'common usage' may be divorced from real meanings in the first
case, or may be related to idiosyncratic understandings in the second.
In both cases definitions in terms of 'common usage' are rooted in
artificial spatial and temporal limits: they are descriptive and
historical.

Second, definitions obtained from 'common usage' also tend to be
ostensive: that is to say, they involve a process of pointing to
certain empirical variables and stating that these variables together
provide the definition of any particular concept. Most 'common
usage' forms are couched in this style, and the specific references to
unique forms of empirical reality again indicate discourse rooted
in the 'language of sources'.

Finally, the ambiguities involved in using definitions based on
'common usage' lead to their major function being jurisdictional
in nature. They function to mark out territory as belonging to one
or another conceptual area. This sort of disagreement is possible
only within the framework of a taxonomic schema which attempts
to classify the various elements into a useful system of order. Disagreements arise when the 'usefulness' of any particular taxonomy
is questioned. Such taxonomies are based on definitions rooted in
the 'language of sources', which provides their fundamental
sources of primary 'units'.

Secularisation: an example of a social myth

Examples of the propagation of social myths are to be found implicit
in many discussions of the problem of definition in the sociology
of religion as well as modernisation and development. A celebrated
critique of *secularisation* as a sociological concept, along with the
suggestion that its use be dispensed with in sociology, has been
made by David Martin (1969b).

Martin wishes to demolish the concept of secularisation by at-
tacking its roots in the definition of the religious. He is concerned
with the 'conventional' (common) usage of religion which, if used
at all, requires secularisation to 'be employed in ways rather far

5

removed from its normal connotation, insofar as the word is employed at all outside the technical context'. However, says Martin, this should not imply a move to analytic definitions because of the danger that they will 'contribute so gross a violation of conventional usage as to arouse constant misunderstanding' (Martin, 1969b:15ff).

The two elements of the saliency aspect outlined above are well illustrated in these remarks. 'Conventional usage' is identified with some undefined but presumably generally available definition, while 'normal connotation' in its technical sense relates to its significance for the groupings in society, again unidentified but presumably theological and sociological in definition. But to which society is Martin referring? By implication it is contemporary society which provides the commonly found definition, and contemporary theologians and sociologists who use it in a technical sense. Hence the mythical aspect of the 'common usage' debate. Obviously a definition rooted in the 'language of sources' will function primarily to mark out territory. As Spiro (1969) points out, such definitions 'are jurisdictional disputes over the phenomenon or range of phenomena which are considered to constitute legitimately the empirical referent of the term.'

The first part of Martin's article, which investigates the oscillation between conventional usage and analytic definitions, is a prime example of the ostensive aspect of the social myth. Each analytic possibility is empirically tested and found wanting, as Martin points to yet another collection of empirical variables which he wishes to include in his definition. The criterion for their inclusion is that of non-violation of conventional usage. Then, when he moves on to discuss conventional definitions, he points again to empirical variables which he feels should be included. In both cases his point of reference is a concept of religion (and hence secularisation) rooted in the 'language of sources'. It is therefore no surprise that he finds contradictions between his conceptualisations and other conceptualisations, or between the conceptualisations themselves.

The mythical element of definitional problems rooted in the language of sources is well understood by Spiro. His definition also has its ostensive, jurisdictional and salient aspects:

> Since 'religion' is a term with historically rooted meanings, a definition must satisfy not only the criterion of cross-cultural applicability but also the criterion of intra-cultural intuitivity; at least, it should not be counter-intuitive. For me, therefore, any definition of religion that does not include, as a key variable, the belief in superhuman ... beings who have power to help or harm man is counter-intuitive (Spiro, 1969:91).

But in each case these have been specified and the nature of the problem associated with them discussed. It is possible to disagree with Spiro, but it is necessary to accept his attempt to justify his approach. It is possible to dismiss it as based on an individual conventional usage rooted in the language of sources. But to consider this as the only proper way to formulate sociological definitions would be to propagate the social myth. All definitions must be related to the reality they define. To suggest that common usage is therefore the *only* guide to satisfactory definition is erroneous.

Social myths are based on the acceptance of reified categories produced outside sociological analysis without recognising them as such. Hence the preoccupation in much Western sociology with the institutionalised aspects of 'religiosity'. The assumption is that, since a common usage definition of Christianity, for example, is concerned with church attendance, membership and presence at rites of passage, these constitute significant elements of a definition of religion, and that any move away from this institutional partici-pation involves religious decline.

This conception of the secularisation process only indicates the extent to which reification can become the basis for facile and misplaced analysis. The error of identifying religiosity in its institu-tional manifestations with a sociological conceptualisation con-stitutes an example of the saliency aspect of social mythology, and limits investigation to the Judaeo-Christian tradition which con-ventionally emphasises this form. The ostensive and jurisdictional aspects combine to facilitate identification. However, such a reified view necessitates the equation of any deviation from a common usage definition with decline. The error of identifying change with decline can occur only when using the language of sources.

Worsley (1968:31) notes that sociologists tend to distinguish be-tween 'natural' and 'supernatural' aspects of religion in a way 'that is not necessarily present in the minds of the believers themselves'. David Martin also notes this tendency to dichotomise in terms of sacred-profane, or this and other-worldly aspects. The average hol-der of religious faith does not stress its supernatural aspects con-tinuously, even though they may contribute a significant element in any 'common usage' definition. 'For most believers, most of the time, the other competences of religion may be quite predom-inant, and are not necessarily anything to do with the supernatural specifically', says Worsley. To suggest that this is not the case is to succumb to social myth-making, for it is only by utilising received definitions located in specific historical realities that such errors arise. It is necessary to understand that the salient aspects of religion are differentially distributed both structurally and temporally, and that 'common usage' can have a variety of meanings dependent upon the location of any specific 'common usage'.

The differential and structural distribution of conceptions of religion can be overlooked by sociologists unaware of the possibility of social myth-making. More specifically there is a theological and historical tradition which identifies the formulators of a religious tradition as mirroring the religious tradition of the society in which they live. Worsley, for example, in noting this problem, asks whether we would accept that a Professor of Theology adequately mirrored the religious values of our society. His answer is negative, but the recent literature in America concerning 'the decline' of religion and religiosity is based on just such views of the significance of the 'God is Dead' debate in theology. Worsley rightly suggests that:

> It is necessary always to distinguish who they are, who says what in what situation, and what the task orientation of the various actors in the situation is, for religion – in the form of esoteric ritual, lore and theology – is differentially distributed throughout society, or elements of it will be differentially distributed or occur only in specific situations, contexts and 'niches', or be available differentially to different actors (Worsley, 1968:xxxiv).

Finally, the problem of idealisation is one common to all sociologists. It is based on the familiar difficulty of differentiating between the observer's and the participant's view of a situation. R. K. Merton (1968:191ff) discusses the convert who became 'over-zealous' in his conformity to the norms and values of his group. Part of the reason, of course, lies in motivation, but another perhaps more important part stems from the want 'of having had first-hand knowledge of the nuances allowable and patterned departures from the norms of the group which he has lately joined'. He also notes that different social structures have, as a result, differing degrees of 'visibility', and that in 'some cases there are internal structural pressures specifically resisting full visibility' (p. 397).

In discussing religion and secularisation this becomes important, since both concepts are mainly rooted in historical reality. Secularisation involves comparison with periods where empirical data is generally limited, and for which an idealised common usage definition of religion provides a basis (see Glasner, 1975). Thus David Martin (1969b:36) talks of a 'Utopian Metaphysics' concerning an ultimate harmony achieved through the 'unveiling of truth' rooted in a Catholic Utopia which identified the thirteenth century as a period when men were 'really religious'. This sort of gross distortion, as Martin himself implies, can only stem from a common usage definition of religion.

Mythology therefore subtly insinuates itself into much sociological analysis of the concepts of religion and secularisation. Its pernicious character lies in a generally unconscious acceptance of the primary or conventional over sociological (that is, *theoretical*) definitions within this particular field.

The notion of secularisation necessarily involves an understanding of the concept of religion, since it is primarily a term used to designate change in that sphere. A variety of closely argued analyses of religious change are available in the literature. These often provide a focus and starting point for discussion which extend the initial arguments (and evidence) beyond permissible bounds. Some sociologists (as well as theologians and religious functionaries) have accepted these extensions at face value.

The concept of secularisation, originating in limited spatial and temporal contexts, has often been widely translated by this process into discussions of contemporary industrial capitalism. Its inclusion in such discussions is often polemical. Attempts are made to use secularisation as part of an ideological critique. On the conservative side it is seen as a contributory factor in the general 'massification' of culture and society (Bell, 1960); it is viewed, from a more radical perspective, as an anti-religious ideology in the guise of Marxism, existentialism or psychoanalysis (Martin, 1969b). It has, therefore, attained a mythological significance in the study of society similar to that of scientific myths in the natural sciences.

Theories of secularisation, then, are typically used to legitimate myths about the decline in moral standards in contemporary life. By doing so they tend to become divorced from their original coordinates of space and time, and hence appear to justify notions for which they had little or no relevance at the outset. They are used to deal with questions of a purely normative kind. It is this aspect that provides the clearest indicator of the presence of social myths in general including modernisation, and of the secularisation myth in particular.

It therefore becomes possible to specify some of the criteria by which the myth-making process can be identified. It is necessary to look, as Toulmin notes, at the question that the myths are being used to answer. It is also necessary to see whether the concepts are being used in more ways than originally intended. Further:

If a conception, however scientific its birth of ancestry, is used in practice only as a way of dealing with non-scientific questions,

9

whether ethical, philosophical or theological – then it is no longer following the trade of its forefathers, and has ceased itself to be a scientific term at all. Again there are some terms of irreproachably scientific origin which begin after a time to lead double lives: as well as their primary scientific metier they acquire part-time jobs of another kind. If we find evidence of such duplicity, our suspicions will be confirmed (p. 17).

For the purposes of this analysis, Toulmin's criteria can be slightly modified by amalgamation, since distortion or extension of a concept's original meaning is not so very different from the addition of new meanings to that concept. New meanings are rarely completely divorced from the old.

In conclusion, the three main criteria for recognising the existence of the process of social mythification are:
(a) seeing whether a concept is being used ideologically;
(b) seeing whether the meaning of the concept can become extended or distorted by *additional* usage;
(c) seeing whether a question being answered related *directly* to the concept used to answer it.

It would seem that by following these criteria at least one major concept in contemporary sociology, that of secularisation, can be described as a social myth. Certainly it has been used by anti-religious ideologies to attack traditional religious forms, and by pro-religious ones to defend them. Specific analyses are taken out of context, and their conclusions extended or distorted in order to bolster these attacks. Finally, secularisation is used as an all-purpose explanation for many of the supposed ills of contemporary society.

The problem of definition

Following Yinger (1971) it is possible to distinguish between valuative definitions which describe what religion 'really' or 'basically' is or ought to be, and substantive definitions which designate certain kinds of beliefs and practices as religion but do not evaluate them. Mythological definitions will be more likely to fall into the category of valuative rather than substantive definitions. This is not to say they are in no way substantive, but rather to suggest that a recognition of their valuative elements would bypass the difficulties involved.

This analysis poses the question: what should a sociological definition of religion look like? Hempel (1952) identifies 'real' and 'nominal' forms of definition in the empirical sciences. The nominal definition of a term is 'a convention which merely introduces an alternative – and usually abbreviated – notation for a given linguistic expression, in the manner of a stipulation'. It has to satisfy one basic requirement: the elimination of the term in favour of the new expression whose meaning is already understood. However, nominal definitions are generally arbitrary in nature, and hence open to debate, though consensus is, in principle, easily obtainable.

A real definition is 'conceived of as a statement of the "essential characteristics" of some entity, as when a man is defined as a rational animal, or a chair as a separate, movable seat for one person' (Hempel, 1952:2). It differs from a nominal definition in that it is concerned with already accepted expressions and their meanings, and does not introduce new ones. It may be empirical or analytic, though it depends on a uniformity of usage which is determined for each user.

Bierstedt notes: 'We judge nominal definitions, in short, by their utility; real definitions by their truth' (1959). Discussing the work of the Committee on Conceptual Integration of the American Sociological Society, whose primary function was to encourage sociologists to adopt uniform nominal definitions, he goes on:

> By no stretch of the imagination, however, can such co-operative endeavour succeed in establishing uniform *real* definition of sociological concepts. In order to arrive at real definition . . . it is necessary to leave the level of verbal equivalent and enter the field of sociological research. When we seek real definition of any sociological concept we no longer want to know what the word stands for, in terms of other symbols, but what the referent of the concept actually is, and what its properties are especially those properties that enable us to use this word, with its own independent meaning, as a terminological and logical equivalent (Bierstedt, 1959:131).

Much of the discussion in social myth is based on nominal rather than real definitions. The process of secularisation itself seems to provide a good example. By suggesting that the religious situation is getting worse rather than better, and applying the term to a variety of changes in that sphere, sociologists confound the arbitrary with the empirically verifiable. Social myths often arise when the concepts investigated are nominally defined because, as already noted, such definitions introduce alternative expressions for specific processes. These expressions often have particular meanings of their own which extend or alter the original conception.

Although originally written at the turn of the century, Simmel's summary of the problem of definition in the sociology of religion still has force today.

> The ambiguity which surrounds the origin and nature of religion will never be removed so long as we insist upon approaching the problem as one for which a single word will be an 'open sesame'. Thus far, no one has been able to offer a definition which, without vagueness and yet with sufficient comprehensiveness, has told once and for all what religion is in its essence, in that which is common alike to the religious of the Christians and South Sea Islanders, to Buddhism and Mexican Idolatry. Thus far it has not been distinguished, on the one hand from mere metaphysical speculation, nor on the other, from the credulity which believes in 'ghosts' (Simmel, 1957).

Contemporary confusion about the actual constituents of a religion can be seen to stem from the same roots as the social myth of secularisation. Confucianism may be described either as a religion or a philosophy of life, while Communism is perhaps as much a religion as a social revolutionary movement (see discussions in Robertson, 1970; Hill, 1973; Towler, 1974).

In some cases, important cultural highspots, such as coronations (Shils and Young, 1953), or Memorial days (Warner, 1962), are described as having a religious significance, while, in others, sporting events are seen as part of contemporary religious life (Cohen, 1964; Coles, 1975).

Cohn (1969) has suggested that at least three possible meanings of religion are available to the sociologist. The most obvious is related to the conventional definition of religion, and is a historical category normally called a Church. Second, there are groupings in society which are not necessarily defined as religious by their members, but whose behavioural characteristics (in the case, for example, of Russian Communists) have much in common with groupings in the first category. Finally, there is the category which is not seen as an institutional grouping by its members, but is unified as such by relating the behaviour of its members to a specific sociological conception of religion. This would be true in the case of the coronation or game of baseball.

Forms of the secularisation process can best be classified according to their origins in the various definitions of religion (Robertson, 1970). However, this approach focuses on the possibility that the operational definition (that is the one actually used in describing the secularisation process) may differ somewhat from the definition expounded in the general discussion of religion. The categories used will approximate to the three areas outlined by Cohn. The secular-

TABLE 1.1 *Major basis of definition of religion*

CATEGORY I (*primarily institutional*)	CATEGORY II (*primarily normative*)	CATEGORY III (*primarily cognitive*)
Type of secularisation process		
1 Decline	1 Transformation	1 Segmentation
2 Routinisation	2 Generalisation	2 Secularisation
3 Differentiation	3 Desacralisation	(Industrialisation)*
4 Disengagement	4 Secularism	(Urbanisation) * (Modernisation)*

* 'Logics' underpinning Category III, Number 2 above.

isation process can be classified according to whether the definition of religion upon which it is based has a primarily institutional, normative or cognitive root. These distinctions, which are principally analytic, will not be used exhaustively. Only the *major* discussions of the secularisation process will be categorised. Not all of these will be explored in any great detail, though at least one from each category will be discussed at some length.

Each major theory has been labelled in an attempt to reflect, as accurately as possible, the process being categorised. The nomenclature is not entirely arbitrary, and has been borrowed, in many instances, from contemporary accounts, (e.g. Shiner, 1967; Schneider, 1970). However the specific meanings attached to these terms are not necessarily reproduced, and some labels have been attached to processes that other authors describe in rather different ways. Table 1.1 illustrates the classification system.

The relationship between the theoretical model of religion which is used to initiate research into secularisation and the ways in which religion is operationalised is not a direct one. The model necessarily delimits the variety of possible operational definitions, although it may not do so in ways which reflect its common usage counterparts. Hence a significant source of error can be located in the disjunction between a substantive definition derived from a specific theoretical perspective, and an attempt to operationalise it in conventional terms. Common usage definitions are only coincidentally similar to theoretically-rooted ones; there exists no *logical* connection (Willer and Willer, 1973).

The next section will be concerned to explicate, in greater detail, the various theories of the secularisation process suggested above.

Each major category will be explored to identify the specific ways in which empirical material becomes distorted in the process of myth-making. In order to clarify each category, an example of the process involved will be isolated and explored in depth.

2 Processes of secularisation

(a) Institutionally based

This chapter is concerned with an exposition of the aspects of the social myth of a secularisation process in which the definition of religion used is rooted primarily in the institutional sphere. The processes outlined below and labelled decline, routinisation, differentiation and disengagement, represent some of the most pervasive forms of this particular myth, mainly because of the ease with which change can be identified in the institutional sphere. Only one, decline, will be discussed in any great detail. However routinisation will also be considered as this process appears to be double-sided, in that two kinds of secularisation process are subsumed by it, one pointing in an opposite direction to the other.

Decline

Although a very popular secularisation thesis, the 'decline' of religion is almost invariably associated with its institutional manifestation. The pioneering studies of Middletown (Lynd and Lynd, 1929, 1937), for example, seize upon the identification of religion and Christianity by Middle-towners themselves ('Middletown does not always stop to think what a religion is. It accepts the word automatically as synonymous with Christianity ...') to conclude that the secularisation process can relate properly only to the church (Lynd and Lynd, 1929:322). They note the existence of forty-two religious groups – and concentrate investigation on the major Protestant ones. Decline is measured by such indices as the secularisation of the Sabbath with the introduction of sport and entertainment, beliefs (relating specifically to those based on the Bible), membership, attendance, Sunday School attendance, church marriages, and so on. The only real attempt to face the problem of religion comes in a brief passage near the end of Part V:

> But if religious life as represented by the churches is less pervasive than a generation ago, other centres of 'spiritual' activity are growing up in the community. However much the ideal or 'service' in Rotary and other civic clubs may be subordinated to certain other interests, these clubs, nevertheless, marked sources of religious loyalty and zeal to some of their members; 'civic loyalty', 'magic Middletown' as a religion appears to be the greatest driving power for some citizens. (Lynd and Lynd, 1929:407).

The secularisation myth has developed strongly on the basis of the studies similar to this, and, although magic is introduced as an alternative to religion in this case, even the word 'magic' is equated mainly with the remedies for bodily ailments, and the possibility of a flourishing Black Magic cult is never explored. They conclude that 'like art and music, religious observances appear to be a less spontaneous and pervasive part of the life of the city today . . .' and identify this with the secularisation process (Lynd and Lynd, 1929:343; see also chapter XXV).

Formal church participation and involvement also constitute the main variables in Lipset's (1963) review of religion in America. He begins his analysis by noting the seeming inconsistency between an increase in adherence to formal religion, as evidenced by much of the statistical material, and the generally accepted sociological view that American religion is highy secularised. In order to resolve this difficulty, Lipset argues that a thorough review of available sources indicates the falsity of the interpretation of a large proportion of the statistical studies.

Lipset notes that early social commentators such as de Tocqueville and Martineau, were agreed that Christianity flourished in America as nowhere else. In order to find statistical backing, Lipset (1963:143ff) goes back to the 1830s for data on membership and adherence, and finds almost universal adherence with a relatively low level of actual membership due mainly to the restrictions surrounding it.

By 1890, 92 per cent of the population were linked to a denomination. Between 1850 and 1900, the proportion of the total population who became members of the various denominations rose only from 15 per cent to 36 per cent. Using the number of effective clergy as a guide, in 1850 there were 1·16 clergymen per 1,000 population, and by 1960 this figure had dropped to 1·13 (in sharp contrast, notes Lipset, with other professional groups). However, most of the evidence pointing to a high degree of institutional religiosity comes from statutes of church membership,[1] and Lipset details many of the drawbacks associated with this index in terms of differential conceptions of the meaning of 'membership'.

Lipset concludes that much of the data shows small 'ebbs and flows' with no basic long-term changes occurring. Certainly the increase in membership figures cannot be taken as indicating a religious revival.

Stark and Glock (1968) who take the investigation a step further, both in scope and time, and by using their dimensional analysis, find America on the verge of a 'Post-Christian era'. A major feature of American Christianity is the continuing erosion of Christian religious beliefs.

> Of course rejection of the supernatural tenets of Christianity is not a modern phenomenon. Through the ages men have challenged these beliefs. But they have never found appreciable support. Until, now, the vast majority of people have remained unshaken in their faith in the other-worldly premises of Christianity (Stark and Glock, 1968 : 205).

To this they add evidence of 'denomination-switching' from those who 'have retained unswerving commitment to that [Christian] faith' to denominations which hold more demythologised views. Attendance is age-related to a large extent, and Stark and Glock quote a Gallup-poll finding showing a drop in weekly attendance of 11 per cent between 1958 and 1966 which they link with those aged less than 50. It is those of 50-plus who most consistently hold 'orthodox' Christian beliefs, and the age division, according to the investigators, is more apparent.

The ecumenical movement, the popularity of literature and debate concerning 'Death of God' theology and the Vatican Council, are also taken as indicators of the 'general corrosion of commitment' which threatens traditional religious views. Hence Stark and Glock are unimpressed by Lipset's statistical manipulation. If secularisation cannot be shown to occur through declining membership, then at least declining church attendance, and increasing denomination switching seem strong indicators that such a process is occurring.

The influence of the Lynds can be seen in the persistent identification of the secularisation of religion with the changes in the institutions of the Christian church.[2] This 'church-oriented religion' to use the phrase coined by T. Luckmann in *The Invisible Religion* (1967), is generally found less significant in urban rather than rural areas, though there seems to be a long-term trend in the decline of church-oriented religion in rural areas as well. However, this ap-

17

proach is not restricted to studies of religion in America. Because of the more obvious changes, it is particularly popular in Europe, and can also be found, to some extent, in analyses of the place of religion, especially the so-called new religions in Japanese industrial society.[3]

The main exponent in Britain is Bryan Wilson,[4] and secularisation is seen by him as the 'process whereby religious thinking, practice and institutions lose their social significance' (Wilson, 1966:xiv). The major variables in his analysis refer primarily to the formal church organisation – religious practice, denominationalism, ecumenicalism, and the liturgical movement.

The statistical evidence for the pattern of secularisation in England shows the decline of the Anglican church since the Industrial Revolution. Wilson uses infant baptism, confirmation, marriage, Sunday School population, Sunday School teachers, enrolments, Easter communicants and membership as indices, concluding that two trends can be discerned:

> the first is the diminution in religious participation over the period of some sixty or seventy years in most forms of religious involvement which amount to more than one isolated ceremonial occasion. The other is the diminution in religious participation over the life cycle of the individual (Wilson, 1966:10).

Denominationalism is placed in the mainstream of the development of individual social experience stemming from the Reformation. Wilson accepts that each new denominational birth indicates religious revival, but argues that it is evidence of the secularisation process none the less.

> As Catholicism was associated with a feudal society and its values, so the various deviations of religious belief and practice, which subsequently found acceptance and became institutionalised, reflected and prompted new interpretations of society and its morality, of theology and of man's responsibility on earth (Wilson, 1966:26).

Revivalism, says Wilson, merely represented a hopeless desire to return to the agrarian social pattern of medieval feudal society, especially during the painful early period of industrialisation. However, because the new religious groupings are not based on kin relations, the values which they espouse become disseminated. In modern, industrialised Britain, with high levels of social and geographical mobility, even denominational allegiance has been found to weaken (Wilson, 1966: chapter 10).

The weakness of denominations in modern England is best

shown, according to Wilson, by the ecumenical movement. This is seen as a specific example of the more general hypothesis that 'organisations amalgamate when they are weak rather than when they are strong, since alliance means compromise and amendment of commitment'. The clerical profession, who provide evidence for the declining status of religion through their declining number and increasing age, see ecumenicalism as the 'new faith' (Wilson, 1966: chapter 5). With their vested interests, says Wilson, they prefer religious alliance to the extinction of religion.

Finally, the development of the liturgical movement, sponsored by the clergy, serves to re-establish the concept of professional monopoly by emphasising the antiquity, legitimacy and performance of the religious role. Combined with episcopacy it helps ensure the maintenance of religion in a nominal position of high esteem. Wilson concludes that this combination of indicators suggests that 'secular society has little direct regard for religion'. However, the identification of religion with its institutional forms in England is recognised by Wilson as constituting the 'commonsense usage of the term' (Wilson, 1966: xvii).

In Japan, the problem of identifying formal membership of religious institutions proves to be extremely difficult. Ministry of Education figures show that the combined membership of Shinto, Buddhism and the new sects far exceeds the population of Japan. Fujio Ikado (1968) suggests that this is due on the one hand to the Shinto custom of regarding all the population of a particular area as being followers, and on the other, to the traditional Japanese affiliation to more than one religious organisation, However, he admits that, on the surface at least, Japan provides a fine example of a highly religious country. The rise of the new sects as *Soka Gakkai*, and *Rissho Koseikai*, would seem to reflect a surging religious revival among the urban population after the initial effects of industrialisation, which seemed to destroy the traditional folk religions. In overall terms, however, there has been a decline in religiosity with the advent of urbanisation and industrialisation, and the new religious movements appear to mark a return to the peace and tranquillity associated with traditional Japanese folk religions (MacFarland, 1967).

These studies have in common the identification of religion with 'church-oriented' religion and the utilisation of conventional definitions of religious institutions. This has had two main results:
(a) difficulties have arisen about when, exactly, the decline in religion began (and, concomitantly, in what state of religion was society when it did); and

19

(b) are the measures used valid or reliable indicators of this form of secularisation?

Views concerning the starting date of religious decline vary. Lipset, for example, seems to suggest that the high point religiosity in America was in the mid-nineteenth century. Wilson sees the church of medieval Europe in this role, while, in Japan, most commentators see the highest levels of religiosity (related to traditional folk religion) at the beginning of this century. David Martin (1969b) has argued that the most common view, certainly in Europe, lies in an Utopian conception of feudal Christianity. It is Utopian because no hard data is available to confirm the hypothesis that the forms of religiosity referred to were in any way more prevalent at that time than in the present day. Gabriel le Bras (1963) has pointed out that during this earlier period the element of compulsion was present, and that talk of 'de-christianisation' becomes meaningless when present day religiosity lies in individual hands. He warns commentators to be wary of the idea of a Christian France before 1789, and suggests it is a myth created by the Romantics, and notes, 'Pour être déchristianisé, il faut bien qu'elles [les populations entières] aient été un jour christianisées.'

T. Luckmann (1967:24) suggests that a major advantage of this identification between church and religion is that it 'legitimates the transfer of the techniques of institutional analysis in the study of the problem'. This has prompted some extreme comments. H. Harmon in Vernon (1962:246) discussing *Religious Behaviour* by Michael Argyle, calls the result 'one more curiosity piece in the museum of quantified studies, a carefully constructed irrelevance', while A. M. Greeley (1970), talking of *Religion in Secular Society*, by Bryan Wilson, notes that this is 'a most naive exposition of the secularisation hypothesis for which one could wish'.

Church membership, perhaps the most commonly used indicator, is a poor measure of religiosity for a number of reasons. Very often the data depend upon the voluntary co-operation of the various church or denomination leaders, who may prohibit their publication, or who do not keep registers.

'Membership' is differentially understood amongst the principal religious institutions, who use indices ranging from baptism to background and culture. Generally it is the well established institutions which provide this sort of information, and many smaller and newer sects may not appear, for example, in the statistics. The classification of sects and denominations is often difficult, with divisions being due as much to language, social class, region or ritual as to theological differences. Finally membership says nothing about the large proportion who are not members of any church:

since these often form a sizeable minority, if not the majority, membership is unlikely to provide a direct measure of overall religiosity (see Petersen, 1962).

Other indicators used in the study of the decline of religion are subject to similar drawbacks (Krausz, 1972). Opinion poll statistics are notoriously unreliable (B. Martin, 1968). Questions such as: Do you believe in God? are open to such broad interpretations that, for example, some 95 per cent of Americans can affirm such a belief (quoted in Lipset, 1963). Attendance relates specifically to the dogma of the particular church, sect or denomination to which the individual adheres, so that, for example, comparisons between Roman Catholics and Protestants along these lines become invalid. Knowledge of the scriptures is also a poor guide, and very often it is the least 'religious' in any sect who are the most knowledgeable in this field.

More general factors, such as ecumenicalism and the liturgical movement, often tend to ambiguity, and can be variously interpreted: for example, ecumenicalism can be interpreted as an index of the strength, rather than the weakness, of denominational religion, since no abrogation of purpose given 'from above' is necessary. Ecumenicalism can be based on an interchange between units sufficiently powerful to allow it. Similarly, the liturgical movement among the clergy may reflect the increasing religious importance of religious institution, and a move away from the social welfare aspects of secularised, church-oriented religion (see discussion in A. M. Glasner, 1970).

Finally, the question of assessing the relationship between the indicators and religiosity itself is generally accepted as problematic. N. J. Demerath (1965) points out that involvement in church-oriented religion can vary in degree and in kind, and any attempt to analyse either aspect must be rooted in theoretical as well as empirical credibility. Thus some individuals may find it in their interest to appear religious without religion significantly informing their inner lives. To this may be added the most important point of all in relation to the decline thesis: that the various measures of religiosity in church-oriented religion need not provide a unitary whole. Thus while church practice may decline, religious beliefs and experiences can remain constant, or even increase. This aspect will be explored in greater detail and with special reference to social class, under the discussion entitled 'permeation'.

Interpretation of the significance of decline in church-oriented religion does not necessarily conclude that secularisation is occurring in any general sense. Shiner (1967) suggests that deviation

21

from traditional forms of religiosity does not necessarily mean an overall decline. He asks:

> Is 'liberal' theology really an adulteration of the historical faith? Or may it not be, as the best liberal theologians have always insisted, an interpretation of the essence of the tradition in the full forms and language of today?

Unfortunately, the decline thesis is not equipped to provide an answer because it rests on an historic, conventional definition of the 'really religious' of doubtful veracity. By implication, all change which constitutes a quantitative decrease in religiosity according to the measures used also involves a qualitative decline. In this respect secularisation, seen as the decline of religion in society, falls prey to conventional usage, and substantiates its status as a social myth.

Routinisation

The term routinisation has been given to the form of secularisation based on the fundamental Weber-Troeltsch dichotomy of church and sect (Weber, 1930; Troeltsch, 1931). This provided an ideal-typical continuum for the analysis of religious organisation. Troeltsch, however, was particularly aware of the limitations which it imposed upon empirical data, and included a third category: mysticism.

The church is defined as a limiting case; it is seen as an integral part of the existing social order. Troeltsch's formulation was rooted specifically in Christianity, and his idea of what constituted the church was linked closely with medieval Catholicism. The sect rejects compromise with the demands of church and society. It is an instrument of social change, and regards religious experience as essentially personal and individual. Werner Stark (1967) has described it as 'typically a contraculture'. The church is large, bureaucratic, and compromises with the world while the sect is small, personal and non-compromising.

Niebuhr (1954) felt that sects would, in time, tend to lose their peculiar socio-ethical characteristics through a general process of routinisation, and a necessary coming-to-terms with the world, purely in order to survive as distinctive groups. He called the survivors of these processes denominations, but in doing so altered the emphasis of the Troeltschian conception of church. Von Wiese and Becker (1932) called this conception the 'ecclesia', and introduced the concept of the cult as the extreme form of private and personal religious organisation. The denominations became 'sects in an advanced state of development and adjustment to each other and to the secular world'.

A large number of extensions have been made of this typology. A recent major attempt to provide a comprehensive classification was made by Milton Yinger (1957) who distinguished six steps:

1　The universal church[5] – which 'combines both church and sect tendencies in a systematic and effective way'. It is not likely to occur often or last long. The best illustration is the Catholic church of the twentieth century.

2　The ecclesia – 'less successful than the universal church in incorporating the sect tendencies'. It becomes more successful in fulfilling its other religious functions.

3　The class church or denomination – 'still less successful in achieving universality than the ecclesia', because it does not withdraw completely from the social order, and is often limited by class, race or region.

4　The established sect – a 'stable' sect which has been 'moulded into a more formidable structure with techniques for admitting new members and preserving their common interests'. This relates specifically to such groups as the Methodists or Quakers.

5　The sect – basically the same as the concept developed by Troeltsch, with further subdivisions into acceptance, aggression and avoidance forms of sectarian response.

6　The cult – 'similar to sects, but represent a sharp break, in religious terms, from dominant religious traditions of society'. It is more likely than the sect to develop around a charismatic leader, and hence tends to form neither an established sect nor a denomination.

This six-fold classification forms a continuum according to two criteria: 'the degree of inclusiveness of the members of the society, and the degree of attention to the function of social integration as contrasted with the function of personal need'. Generally speaking, the last three should be seen in reverse order, that is, cult–sect–established sect.

H. W. Pfautz (1955) saw 'in order of increasing secularisation' a typology of religious groups ranging from cult and sect at one end to church and denomination at the other, with the established sect as an alternative form of development. Using five sociological frames of reference, the demographic, the ecological, the associational, the structural, and the social psychological, Pfautz analyses the development of Christian Science in his typology. Each frame of reference changes, but not necessarily at the same moment as the others.

His concern is to show how such factors as size, position and rate of growth increased, together with restitution and segregation, with the development of the cult. Other factors used include internal and external differentiation, the basis of interaction and recruitment, and the type of authority and leadership. He concludes, 'beginning in the 1840's Christian Science began to move towards becoming an institutionalised sect', with the reorganisation of the group after the death of its leaders, and the setting up of an hierarchical establishment.

The church is seen by Pfautz as the most developed form of religious social organisation, and hence the best able to survive. He also quotes the Catholic church of the thirteenth century as an example. However, 'the denomination is one extreme form of secularisation process as exemplified by protestant American religious bodies: they are associations rather than communities.' The most religious form of organisation is therefore the cult, mainly because it is also the most elementary. Its survival depends upon a move from primary to secondary social relationships, and its development into a sect. But, by doing so, areas of social interaction which are not specifically religious became necessary adjuncts, and the unanimity of concern begins to disintegrate. Pfautz provides a diagram to illustrate this (see Figure 2.1).

Yinger notes that a cult is almost wholly concerned with 'the problems of the individual'. It is not so much rebelling against the established order, as does the sect, but is *outside* it. Often it is syncretist in nature taking elements from a number of available religious ideas and synthesising them into novel and sometimes bizarre religious forms.[6]

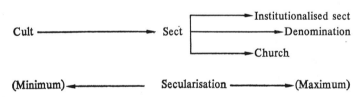

Figure 2.1 Secularisation, according to Pfautz (1955:121)

This has led Nelson (1968:357) to suggest that through institutionalisation 'all founded religions can be said to have developed from cults'. The cult–new religion continuum, he suggests, is a different one altogether from the sect–church continuum. The new religion may exhibit its own churchly or sectarian tendencies (see Yinger, 1971:270–80). Will Herberg (1967) follows Pfautz in suggesting that the cult is the least secularised form of religious group.

His analysis is based on the distinction to be made between three forms of usage of religion:

> One, in the first place 'religion' is properly used for the system of attitudes, beliefs, feelings, standards and practices, that, in the particular society, generally receive the name of religion. For our purposes, we will designate religion in this usage as 'conventional religion'. Two, in the second place, 'religion' may be taken in to signify that the system of attitudes, beliefs, feelings, standards and practices actually does *in fact* provide the society with an ultimate context of meaning and value in terms of which social life are integrated and social activities are validated. This I will call 'the operative religion' of a society. Three, in the third case 'religion' may be understood existentially (Herberg, 1967:470-1).

The process of secularisation, as seen in cultural terms, occurs when 'the conventional religion is no longer the operative religion in the sociological sense but has been replaced by another "set of ideas, rituals and symbols"'. American society provides the example of a country whose culture is in an advanced state of secularisation. 'Denominational pluralism, on the American plan, means through-going secularisation.'

Herberg then goes on to link this continuum with the concept of tri-faith system, developed in his classic: *Protestant–Catholic–Jew* (1955).

> In the American system, denominations have their groupings within a scheme of mutually legitimated coexistence: specifically they group themselves into three great socio-religious sub-communities known as the 'three great faiths'. We can thus carry the series further: *cult–sect–denomination–socio–religious community* (Herberg, 1955:517).

But the Troeltschian concept of the church, when separated from its specific form as an organised institution, appears to correspond to the tri-faith system. Hence a further stage can be added to the typology which now runs: cult–sect–denomination–socio–religious community–tri-faith system. Herberg (1967) concludes: 'Beyond this, secularisation cannot go. In the tri-faith system conventional religion and operative religion have been almost completely separated and almost completely syncretised.'

The view of the secularisation process involved in the above discussion appears in many respects to be a reversal of the decline thesis. Instead of the medieval church providing the high point of religiosity, it is seen as near the secular end of the cult–denomina-

25

C

tion continuum. The difference, of course, rests on the indices used to identify religiosity: fundamentally, institutionalisation is a positive measure in the decline concept of secularisation and the negative indicator is routinisation. These two views represent, as it were, two sides of the same coin. This is, however, a slight over-simplification because of the distinction between church (or ecclesia) and denomination: the latter being recognised as more secular than the former. This provides evidence of another form of secularisation thesis, based on institutional differentiation, to be discussed below.

However, a contradiction does seem present which would indicate that Pfautz's view of the church, as an alternative and less secularised form of development of the sectarian form, may be an inaccurate representation. This contradiction suggests that the denomination, although highly institutionalised, does not appear to accommodate to the existing social order as much as the church. Since there appear to be, with exceptions, similarities between the two concepts in all other areas, it would seem more logical to accept Herberg's typology of cult–sect–denomination–socio-religious community–tri-faith system, as providing a form of the secularising process. It is suggested that the reasons for not doing so lie in Pfautz's non-articulated view that American denominationalism is an example of secularised society *par excellence*. Such a view is in keeping with the overall common usage definitions of religion and secularisation which underlie the analysis particular to the routinisation form of the concept of secularisation.

Differentiation

The Parsonian school provides a good example of the identification of the process of differentiation itself with secularisation. Thus, in describing the 'secularised' society of modern America, Talcott Parsons says:

> Looked at by comparison with earlier forms, religion seems to have lost much. But it seems to me that the losses are mainly the consequence of processes of structural differentiation in the society, which correspond to changes in the character of religious orientation but do not necessarily constitute a loss of strength of the religious values themselves (Parsons, 1960: 320).

This form of secularisation is an implied critique of the decline and routinisation theses. Parsons's argument is that the process of secularisation should be understood as a tendency to give religion a redefined place in the social scene and not as the elimination of organised religion. The keynote, structural differentiation, explains the confusion:

> When a previously less differentiated structure becomes differentiated into more specialised subsystems; it is in the nature of the case that, if an earlier and later structural unit bear the same name, the later version will, by comparison with the earlier, be felt to have lost certain functions, and hence, perhaps, from a certain point of view have been weakened (Parsons, 1960:301).

But structural differentiation has two aspects: the development of pluralistic organisation on the one hand; and the development of 'higher levels of generality' on the other. It is with the former, that this discussion is primarily concerned. The latter aspect is discussed under the heading *generalisation*, the development of generic religion.

The process of structural differentiation occurs in the context of a generalised theory of societal evolution. The paradigm of evolutionary change developed by Parsons is based on the enhancement of adaptive capacity. Units or sub-systems with single, relatively well defined places in society, divide into further units or subsystems, which differ both in structure and in functional significance for the wider system. Parsons notes:

> If differentiation is to yield a balanced more evolved system, each newly differentiated substructure must have increased adapted capacity for performing its *primary* function as compared to the performance of that function in the previous, more diffuse structure (Parsons, 1966:22).

The differentiation between the social community and the religious community, within Christianity itself, and between faith and ethics in the latter, has resulted in the 'endowment of secular life with a new order of religious legitimation'.[7]

R. N. Bellah (1964) provides a more detailed analysis of religious evolution, which he defines as:

> A process of increasing differentiation and complexity of organisation which endows the organism, social system or whatever the unit in question may be, with greater capacity to adapt to its environment so that it is in some sense more autonomous relative to its environment than were its less complex ancestors.

He specifically rejects inevitability and irreversibility as part of his conception, and is willing to accept on empirical grounds the possibility that complex forms can develop into simpler and less complex ones. He feels that, as an empirical generalisation, 'More complex forms develop from less complex forms and that the properties and possibilities of more complex forms differ from their less complex forms.'

Religion is defined as the various symbols and rituals relating man to his ultimate concerns. A number of presuppositions provide the basis of Bellah's analysis:

(a) that religious symbolisation changes over time;
(b) that conceptions of religious action, organisation and a place of religion in society, change in a similar manner as (a); and
(c) that religious evolution is necessarily related to socio-cultural evolution.

The validity of these suppositions is, of course, open to question, and indicates a degree of pre-judgment about the outcome of the secularisation process being discussed. It is suggested that they indicate a stumbling block resulting from the social myth-making.

Bellah's analysis rests on four variables: the religious symbol system; the forms of religious action; the types of religious organisation; and the social implications of changes in these characteristics. These changes are typified in five ideal-type stages, each of which has limited temporal reference: these are primitive; archaic; historic; early modern; and modern religion.

Primitive religious symbolisation is rooted in a mythical world with two important features; it is related to a high degree with the real world, and its organisation is fluid. Religious action is characterised by 'participation' or 'acting out', and religious organisation as a separate social structure does not exist. Bellah suggests that the social implications follow from four main functions developed by Durkheim in *The Elementary Forms of the Religious Life* (1915). Using H. Alpert's (1939) classification these are:

1 Disciplinary and preparatory;
2 Cohesive;
3 Revitalising;
4 Euphoric.

Archaic religion has a mythical symbol system but with a greater degree of characterisation. It is more objectified and more active in relation to world affairs. Religious action takes the form of the cult, with a more definite distinction between men as subjects and gods as objects. Religious organisation is still largely merged with other social structures, but the increasing proliferation of hierarchically differentiated status groups leads to the multiplication of cults. The social implications are again Durkheimian, but the increasing division of labour introduces new roles, and hence novel forms of behaviour and 'new ways of seeing'.

In historic religion, the symbol systems involve transcendentalism and are therefore dualistic. This represents the demythologisation stage of religious evolution, through the simplification of myth. Religious action becomes necessary for salvation, and there emerges a clear concept of the self. Religious organisation involves the emergence of differentiated religious collectivities, with the attendant increase, in the sphere of social implications, of probabilities for tension and conflict.

Religious symbolisation concentrates on the direct relation between the individual and transcendent reality in early modern religion. Religious action is now conceived to be identical with the whole of life. Stress is laid on the internal qualities of the individuals, rather than specifically 'religious' acts. The concept of hierarchy is abandoned in the symbol system and religious organisation operates with a two-fold division between the elect and the reprobate only. Bellah recognises that the social implications can be very complex and cites Weber's (1930) study of the link between Protestantism and Capitalism as an example of the difficulties involved.

In turning to modern religion, Bellah almost paraphrases Parsons' views given above.

> To concentrate on the church in a discussion of the modern religious situation is already misleading, for it is precisely the characteristic of the new religious situation that the great problem of religion as I have defined it, the symbolisation of man in relation to the ultimate condition of his existence, is no longer the monopoly of any groups explicitly labelled religious.

The possibilities of religious symbolisation become infinite because of the Kantian revolution, and, with the disappearance of collective symbolism comes the atrophy of religious organisation as dealing with the specifically religious. There is, however, a continuing search for adequate standards by which to assess the non-empirical aspects of life. Bellah rejects Paine's notion of the identity of mind and church, and suggests that the main function of institutionalised religious groupings is to provide a suitable environment within which the individual formulates his own solutions. Bellah is advocating therefore what amounts to a privatisation of religion within a plurality of institutional groupings, similar to those proposed by Luckmann. The social implications should not be interpreted as a collapse of moral standards, etc., but as offering

29

TABLE 2.1

	Primitive religion	Archaic religion	Historic religion	Early modern religion	Modern religion
A Religious symbolism	Mythical	Mythical, but more objectified	Dualistic	Concentration on relation between individual and transcendent reality	Infinite variation (post-Kant)
B Religious action	Participatory	Cultic, with beginnings of I–Thou differentiation	Salvationist, with clear concept of Self	Religious life identified with 'living'	Continuation of search of adequate standards
C Religious organisation	Non-existent	Largely non-existent (except for status groupings)	Differentiated religious collectivities, with establishment of hierarchies	Reduction of hierarchy with dichotomous view of elect v. reprobate	Disappearance of collected symbolism
D Social implications	Group cohesion, comfort, teaching and social control (cf. Durkheim, 1915)	As in primitive religion, with possibility of new ways of seeing	Possible tension and conflict	Complex (cf. Weber, 1930)	Unprecedented opportunities for creative innovation

Source: Extracted from Bellah (1964).

unprecedented opportunities for creative innovation in all human spheres. A brief summary, extracted from his article, can be found in Table 2.1. This sort of analysis of the secularisation process is open to the major criticism that, for example, Bellah, while dissociating himself from it, is prone to 'metaphysical evolutionism'. By using a definition of evolution involving the development of more complex forms from simpler ones, he sees a necessary teleological purpose in his analysis. Autonomous development of complex forms of religious symbolism are not elaborated, and early forms are defined as 'simple'.

Other elements of 'metaphysical evolutionism' become more apparent on further study. Development is seen as occurring on one plane only: that of differentiation. Hence the 'near autonomy' of the organism from its environment (which Bellah suggests comes with modern religion) is accepted as part and parcel of the process of differentiation. No attempt is made to establish a relationship between these two variables, and no attempt is made why they should 'evolve' at the same rate.

Finally it should be noted that Bellah's 'theory' has little or no predictive power; it is basically a natural history of the aspects of religiosity which he has chosen. Lacking a fundamentally theoretical approach, and falling prey to the limitations of developmentalism (Nisbet, 1970), he can only envisage stages in religious evolution which are made available by historical reality. By using differentiation as his only dynamic, Bellah must, of necessity, remain within the historically defined limits of differentiation. In fact he stops earlier than this by not accepting Paine's 'My mind in my Church'.

Bellah may reply that this theory was only a broad schematic outline. However, by limiting himself to the evolutionary framework and falling prey to the very aspects of 'metaphysical evolutionism' which he denies, Bellah has produced an artificial taxonomy with no theoretical backing and bearing little relation to the reality and diversity of world-wide religious symbolism.

Disengagement

Secularisation is seen as the change from ecclesiastical control to public administration in all aspects of social life. It is concerned with the rise of the secular state and its gradual take-over of most of the activities once performed by religious institutions. Unlike secularism, which is based on a denial of the value of the religious in society, this aspect of secularisation emanates from a desire to

31

disengage certain key aspects of social life and to emancipate them from religious tutelage.

Most of the work in this area relates to changes in the position of Christianity since the Middle Ages. W. Stark (1967) traces what Mehl (1970) calls the 'transfer of the *corpus mysticum* from the Church to the State' in some detail. Here the similarity to secularisation as transformation should be noted. However, a new meaning then develops where the: 'profane world, the world of daily life . . . avoids the influence of the church. It rejects the church's presence and encloses it in a sphere that is clearly differentiated from global society.'

Secularisation is also expressed as a rebellion, manifested in the arts and philosophy, against the limitations of theology. Bacon's recourse to experimentation, the introduction of mathematics to research, and the concept of independent evaluation, all led to a new independence in scientific investigation. Galileo and Descartes only represent examples of the church's rearguard action in the field of these new and 'entirely secularised' physical sciences. The developments in science were paralleled by the secularisation of human sciences and of political life, although this latter process was often delayed after the Reformation, for example, until quite recently in such countries as Spain and Italy (see, for example, Hazard, 1953).

In a fully secularised state a man can be born, received into a family, educated, married, be able to work and receive honours, and finally to die, all without recourse to institutional religious forms. The difference between disengagement and secularisation seen as decline lies in the fact that religious institutions still exist in the former case, though not necessarily as an intrusive element in social life, while in the latter case they have simply atrophied out of existence. In a society secularised through disengagement, religion is able to return to its 'true nature'.

This process has also been isolated in the growth of some non-European secular states. Donald E. Smith (1963) argues that the adoption of religious neutrality by the Indian government after the introduction of its new constitution is an example of such disengagement. Other cases studied include the rise of Ataturk's Turkey (Berkes, 1964; Bellah, 1958), Japan (Bellah, 1958), and, of course, the USA (Parsons, 1958; Yinger, 1971:436–56).

One specific form of this process of secularisation can be found in the French development known as 'laïcité'. W. Bosworth (1962) admits to a certain degree of ambiguity in this term, especially in its overlap with the notion of 'secularism'. It certainly involves 'the separation of spiritual matters from the competence of the State', though he quotes Cardinal Gerlier as saying:

> Laicité of the state can have quite varied meanings. If it concerns an affirmation of the sovereign authority of the state in its domain of temporal order ... this doctrine is fully in accord with that of the Church ... If Laicité of the state means that, in a country of many beliefs, the state should allow each citizen to practice freely his religion, this second meaning, if correctly understood also conforms to Church doctrine.

Bosworth concludes that laicité is best understood as a doctrine of complete freedom and non-interference for religion.

The emancipation from ecclesiastical tutelage has its roots in Renaissance Humanism, and more especially, the Enlightenment. It was during this last period that the intrinsic value of the world was initially recognised in all spheres, and outright autonomy from religion was sought (Niermann, 1970:70; Dansette, 1961, vol. II; Boulard, 1960).

In France, the constitutional separation of church and state was only completed under the Third Republic in 1905. The church had already been deprived of support from public funds, and, though freely available for use, church buildings became state property. Religious instruction in state schools had been abolished in 1882 and replaced by general ethical instruction. In 1904 all institutionalised religion was prohibited from any form of teaching. Pius XII coined the phrase 'sound, legitimate laicity' to describe the eventual situation in France, with its autonomous state guaranteeing religious freedom as part of the common good, after the First World War.

The Enlightenment also provoked the final disengagement of philosophical thought during the eighteenth century. Gellner has claimed, with some qualifications, that its major significance was to have forged and formulated the 'main element of the outlook of Western European secularised intelligentsia until this day ...' (Gellner, 1964). It was manifested in the development of a theory of progress based on a 'materialistic' conception of the natural world, and it paved the way for the French Revolution.[8]

The specific problem associated with this form of the secularisation process lies in its necessary generality. Disengagement can occur in both the cultural and structural spheres, and need not be temporally linked. Such changes, when so linked, need not be related, though they may be seen as connected *ex post facto*. The main problem is thus one of establishing any causal links, except in the purely historical sense. It becomes impossible to gauge what

33

the effects of the Enlightenment actually were, given that a certain degree of disengagement had already begun during the Renaissance.

A second problem arises, however, in relation to the development of secularism as a specifically anti-religious ideology. This, too, was the product of the Enlightenment, and the two forms of the secularisation process are necessarily closely interwoven. As a result it is sometimes difficult to judge where disengagement stops and secularism begins. Indeed, the possible coexistence of the two due to a logical interconnection cannot be overlooked. Certainly early definitions of secularism are in terms of a move by the priest out of his total environment into the 'world', which is surely a process of disengagement.

Conclusion

The myth of a secularisation process can be seen to operate clearly when the basis for defining religion (or religiosity) is institutionally bound.

Using the first of Toulmin's criteria, it becomes relevant to ask whether religion continues to flourish outside the structures which have conventionally embodied it. Specific historical situations are used to form the basis of broader generalisations to which they bear only scant resemblance.

In the case of the decline of religion, which has been explored in most detail here, the ideological nature of the discussion is manifested in the insistence that contemporary society is, in some way, necessarily the most secular. Since this view can only be based on the addition of new meanings to the limited (spatial and temporal) analyses which provide the foundation for such a generalisation, it can only be seen as reflecting the preconception of the theorists.

However, the decline of religion provides only one example, and the other three major theories discussed are equally open to criticism on this count.

It is therefore possible to conclude that the theories of the secularisation process classified as originating in definitions of religion, which are primarily structural in nature and institutional in form, have attained a mythical status because of their reliance on conventional usage and ideology. This ideology reflects the pervasive notion of *progress* discussed briefly in relation to modernisation in the introduction. Nisbet (1970: 360–1) makes the point well in his critique of directionality, which, as he notes, 'lies in the mind of the beholder'. A comprehensive discussion of the ideology of progress can be found in Sklair (1970, especially Part I), who traces its roots as far back as Plato and Aristotle.

34

(b) Normatively based

This section is concerned with an exposition of the substantive aspects of the social myth of a secularisation process in which the definition of religion used is rooted primarily in the normative sphere. It will include discussions of generalisation, transformation, desacralisation and secularism, but only generalisation will be explored in any great detail.

Generalisation

This form of secularisation stems, in large part, from the analysis of differentiation outlined in the previous section. However, the emphasis here is not on the pluralistic effects of social differentiation in terms of the institutional aspects of society, but on the generalising effect it has on the over-arching norms and values held in common by that society. Parsons locates religious values in the cultural system and notes that, 'In some sense, all societal values are here conceived analytically as religiously grounded.' He specifically notes that secularisation on the 'collectivity level of structure' does not mean the absence of a religious orientation at the levels of norms and values. In fact, he feels that the confusion caused by this interpretation has led to a misunderstanding the reasons for describing American society as 'secularised' (Parsons *et al.*, 1961).

The differentiation in society has certainly led to a greater diversity of specialised sub-collectivities than found, for example, in the universal church.

> But this process has coincided with the development of *higher* levels of generality in the religious requirements of normal societal membership. For example the societal 'common denominator' is considerably more general than was that of Medieval Catholicism (Parsons *et al.*, 1961:57).

This view is best illustrated with reference to social control. In a traditional society, religious norms and values exercise low level, specific prescriptions regarding behaviour. Almost everything is judged in religious terms, from the details of a woman's cosmetics to the general deportment of the population as a whole. Smelser notes that, under such conditions, dissatisfaction with *social* arrangements automatically becomes a revolt against *religious* ideas. Thus:

> if interest on loans is defined as sinful rather than merely economically unsound, controversy over interest becomes a

religious conflict rather than a matter of economic policy (in Schneider, 1970:62).

Bellah (1958) contrasts this with more modern and differentiated forms of society where:

> an area of flexibility must be gained in economic, political and social life in which the specific norms may be determined in considerable part by short-term exigencies in the situation of action, as by functional requisites of the relevant social subsystem. Ultimate religious values lay down the basic principles of social action . . . the religious system does not attempt to regulate economic, political and social life in great detail . . .'

Schneider argues that, in a differentiated society, some overarching integrative system must be presented in a generalised level, especially in a society like America with its diverse immigrant populations. This does not preclude specific low-level disagreements between the existing groups. (For a discussion of the American creed v. way of life see Myrdal, 1944, and Herberg, 1955.)

Bellah's analysis of Turkey and Japan shows the differentiation of religion and ideology on two distinct levels. In Turkey, the greatest advances in economic, political and social life have been on the cultural foundation of six principles (see Berkes, 1964), but he notes that the political difficulties are still bound up with traditional religious conceptions, so that the move from traditional society may be only temporary. In Japan, on the other hand, the agitation of liberal elements for a complete separation of church and state resulted, in 1889, in the inclusion of a clause guaranteeing religious freedom in the constitution. The official support of state Shinto continued, but it was declared an expression of patriotism rather than a religion. This ideology had, of course, enormous consequences in the 1940s. 'The new 1946 constitution', says Bellah (1958:5), 'by disestablishing Shinto and deriving sovereignty from the people rather than from the sacred and inviolable Emperor, theoretically completed the process of secularisation.'

Herberg (1967a; 1967b) follows his analysis of the tri-faith system and the concept of the 'American way of life' in two later articles, and asserts that the various denominations together form a 'common religion'. Secularisation is defined as the increasing separation (differentiation) of the 'operative religion' of a culture (which provides the society with its ultimate context of meaning and value), from its 'conventional religion' (which provides the general usage of the term). The 'counter-currents' to secularisation include the fundamentalist groups, older ethnic churches, and the growth of sectarian movements for whom the process of differentiation has not yet begun.[9]

Herberg's thesis was foreshadowed by de Tocqueville's *Democracy in America*, in which it was suggested that the Americans worshipped a 'religion-in-general' as far back as the early nineteenth century. P. E. Hammond (1976) discusses its development and argues that the specific aspect of differentiation lies within the ethical sphere. This function has been taken over by the state, whose procedures assume a 'sacred quality'. Hence religions no longer 'inform culture', even though the churches may exercise an ethical influence and perhaps remain primary developers and transmitters of non-empirical beliefs.

The 'common religion' of modern Americans includes the conventional religion of the tri-faith system and the concept of American democracy and the American way. According to Herberg (1967a):

> Secularisation, even in its benign form, means the subversion of the normative relation between religion and culture. Instead of culture standing under the judgement of the God to whom religion witnesses, religion (that is, conventional religion) tends to understand itself as an expression of, and utility for, the culture. It is this kind of benevolent co-existence that accounts for much of the paradox of contemporary American religion – the paradox of the religiousness of society in an advanced state of secularisation.

In this analysis Herberg is in substantial agreement with Parsons.

> Consequently, religion enjoys a high place in the American scheme of things, higher today, perhaps, than at any time in the past century. But it is a religion thoroughly secularised and homogenized, a religion-in-general, that is little more than a civic religion of democracy, the religionisation of the American Way (Knudten, 1967: chapter 46).

R. N. Bellah has extended his general analysis of this specific aspect of the differentiation process and postulated the concept of 'civil religion' in America, which is similar in many ways to those discussed above. He prefers to view it as a 'religious dimension' which exists alongside such conceptions as 'the American way of life'. He notes the separation of church and state and analyses the essential privatisation of religiosity (others include Eckhardt, 1958; Marty, 1959; and Vahanian, 1961), arguing that:

> Although matters of personal religious belief, worship and

association are considered to be strictly private affairs, there
are, at the same time, certain common elements of religious
orientation that the great majority of Americans share. . . .
[They] provide a religious dimension for the whole fabric of
religious life. . . . The public religious dimension is expressed
in a set of beliefs, symbols and rituals that I am calling American
civil religion (Bellah, 1967).

Bellah quotes, as an example, the inauguration of the President.

The initial impetus stemmed from the Declaration of Independence and Thanksgiving Day speeches, the style of which served to shape the 'form and tone' of civil religion as it is today. It built up a set of powerful symbols of national solidarity, and these mobilised those aspects of behaviour relating to the attainment of national goals. The process of differentiation will necessarily mean the development of a super-national civil religion, and Bellah specifically denies that civil religion is the worship of the American nation. The form of this development cannot yet be ascertained. However, civil religion is not simply a 'religion-in-general', because of its necessary American reference.

Precisely because of this specificity, the civil religion was
saved from empty formalism, and served as a genuine vehicle
of national religious self-understanding (Bellah, 1967).

Bellah sees civil religion as the over-arching generic form of religion *in America*, and hence as an example of the process of secularisation *in America*. In principle, the concept of civil religion does remain globally extendable.

This latter point underlines a major problem with the generalisation hypothesis, namely the extent to which it reflects the existing cultural background or the extent to which it is a 'generalised' form of the existing religious conception. It is arguable, for example, that Bellah's idea of a civil religion involves too great an amount of inherited Protestant (or at least Judaeo-Christian) religious ideas. This appears to contrast with Herberg's view of the place of the 'American way of life' which *includes* such conceptions, but only as a part of the whole.

Hence, Herberg's thesis is specifically American, while Bellah's appears specifically Judaeo-Christian. Neither hazard a guess at what a non-Western 'civil' religion would look like, though Bellah does imply that Japanese nationalism forms a good parallel. However, such nationalism would appear to bear a greater similarity to Herberg's conception than to Bellah's. In either case, the usefulness of employing a concept of 'religion' (even in its secularised form) in this context is open to question, unless a completely Durkheimian approach is adopted (a view, it seems, accepted by Parsons), and all integrating value systems are accepted, by definition, as religious.

In addition there is the problem of the actual identification of such highly differentiated generic religions. Where do they cease to be in 'loose control' and begin to influence specific aspects of behaviour? To what extent can such a loosely defined system be said to influence behaviour at all? To what extent are the values of generic religion *actually* held in common by the American public? This leads on to an area of difficulty already encountered in dealing with the 'decline' thesis; namely, the operational drawbacks of religious concepts.[10]

Transformation

Early examples of the transformation of religious values, grounded in divine power, to specifically worldly ones can be found in the work of Weber and Troeltsch. Talcott Parsons, describing the process of secularisation discussed in Weber's *The Protestant Ethic and the Spirit of Capitalism* (1930) suggests that the main element lies in the emancipation of capitalism from ethical control as evidenced by the 'mitigation of ascetic rigour in the latter stages of the development of the Protestant Ethic (Parsons, 1937: 685).

Weber himself mentions it in his analysis of the effect of wealth on monasticism:

> In fact the whole history of Monasticism is in a certain sense the history of continual struggle with the problem of the secularising influence of wealth. The same is true on a grand scale of the worldly asceticism of Puritanism (Weber, 1930: 174–5).

Wealth is the result of the capitalist mode of the appropriation with its emphasis on the 'rational organisation of labour', and modern Western capitalism resulted from the peculiar ethic of ascetic Puritanism.

This ethic reversed the traditionally rational attitude towards the acquisition of money, the concern with satisfaction of material needs. Weber sought the clue to this reversal in the Biblical quotation he found in the works of Benjamin Franklin: 'Seest thou a man diligent in his business? He shall stand before Kings' (Proverbs XXII: 29). As Bendix (1966: 256) notes, Weber outlined the imperative element during his analysis of ancient Judaism where the prophets are seen as 'establishing a new faith subjecting man's

39

daily life to the imperatives of a divinely ordained moral law'. It was the Puritan who interpreted it as a duty or calling.

And in truth this peculiar idea, so familiar to us today, but in reality so little a matter of course, of one's duty in a calling, is what is most characteristic of the social ethic of capitalistic culture, and is in a sense the fundamental basis of it. It is an obligation which the individual is supposed to feel and does feel towards the content of his professional activity, no matter whether it appears on the surface as a utilisation of his personal powers, or only of his material possessions (of capital) (Weber, 1930:54).

This spirit of capitalism was to be found originating in Calvinism, which was identified by its adherents with the 'True Faith'. Election to the Kingdom of Heaven could no longer be identified with any certainty, but good works became the technical means, not so much of certainty of election, as of not being damned. Thus the Calvinist created his own conviction of salvation. 'The God of Calvinism demanded of his believers, not single good works, but a life of good works combined into a unified system' (Weber, 1930:117).

The by-product of this sober and regulated attitude to life was the accumulation of wealth and the development of modern capitalism. But capitalism began to develop a driving force of its own, and its religious roots became transformed into utilitarian worldliness.

Where the fulfilment of the calling cannot be directly related to the highest spiritual and cultural values, or when on the other hand it need not be felt simply as economic compulsion, the individual generally abandons the attempt to justify it at all. In the field of its highest development, in the United States, the pursuit of wealth stripped of its religious and ethical meaning, tends to become associated with purely mundane passions, which often actually give it the character of sport (Weber 1930:182).

Troeltsch (1955) attempted to provide evidence for the theory that religious authority had become transformed in the process leading to the production of the modern state. Protestantism was concerned with individual liberty and independence of thought.

The idea is at first religious. Later it becomes secularised and overgrown by the rationalistic, sceptical and utilitarian idea of toleration. . . . But its real foundations were laid in the English

Puritan Revolution. The momentum of its religious impulse opened the way for modern freedom.

This idea of independence resulted in the development of an autonomous state system, though in its early stages the growing body of officialdom was still invested with 'the character of a God-ordained calling'. But as it grew, and as it became more concerned with the 'advancement of civilisation' (which, according to Troeltsch, also had a religious impetus), the state became the guardian of such aspects of life as education, morality, food – and ultimately spiritual and ethical well-being.[11]

> By the separation of civilisation from the Church, while the civilising functions are retained by the State, there arises the modern idea of the State as an organ of civilisation (Troeltsch, 1955:109).

Troeltsch traces similar signs of the transformation of the religious ethic in the spheres of law, the family, marriage and sex. Thus the 'complete severance of sensual feelings from the thought of original sin', through the newly gained independence of art and poetry, 'has resulted in nothing else than the secularisation of the intense religious emotion'. As with Weber, it is a specific element of Protestant Christianity which becomes the agent of transformation in this form of the secularisation process.[12]

Shiner (1967:215) notes that psychoanalysis and Marxism provide some authorities with other examples of this concept of secularisation although he calls it 'transposition'. Thus Erich Fromm (1950) talks of the former as an outcome of humanistic religion and its concern with the 'cure of the soul'. William Clebsch (1969) suggests that, because of the increasing importance of the criterion of client welfare, two of the traditional roles of the clergyman, healing and guidance, have been respectively taken over by the physician and the psychotherapist. This latter 'therapeutic' element is increasingly focusing the work of the churches into the area of 'dispensing comfort' (discussed in Wilson, 1968). The process of transformation in the work of the founder of psychoanalysis is dealt with by Philip Rieff (1959, 1966). The parallel between religion and psychoanalysis, especially in such areas as the father-figure/analyst, confession/analysis and sin/neurosis, are too well known to need further elaboration here.

Marxism has also been seen as an example of the transformation of the Judaeo-Christian tradition, especially in its eschatological elements. Tucker (1961) notes that it follows the pattern of the great religious conceptions of Western culture. This is evidenced by its

41

D

aspirations to totality of scope, like medieval Christianity; a historical world view, with an Augustinian portrayal of the present as the last historical world-period before judgment/revolution; salvation through the spiritual dealienation of man, and the praxis between theory and action.

Arthur Koestler testifies to the religious quality of Marxism which he likens to a 'mental explosion'.

> There is now an answer to every question, doubts and conflicts are a matter of the tortured past – a past already remote, when one lived in dismal ignorance in the tasteless, colourless world of those who *don't know* (Koestler *et al.*, 1950:23).

Johnson (1961) provides a chart comparing the essential elements of medieval Christianity and Communism. However, the problem here is whether Marxism constitutes a true transformation or is merely as Yinger suggests, a functional alternative.[13]

The problem of *ex post facto* analysis underlies this discussion of the secularisation process. Religious transformation is difficult to predict within the terms of reference of the theory. It remains a descriptive, historical analysis with no real explanatory content.

Identification of the production of transformation, as Shiner notes, is very difficult and depends upon the skill and insight of the investigator, thus making it open to abuse, and rendering the results questionable. Given the historian's use of conventional definitions of religion, problems increase when attempts are made to improve sociological categories which may not coincide with the historical ones, and the relevance of the question of meaning is raised. As Yinger and Shiner note, the question of meaning becomes highly relevant in distinguishing between *transformations* of religion and *functional alternatives* to it. The transformation of religion, seen as a theory of secularisation rests on unstable theoretical and methodological grounds, especially when transformations seem to be concluded within the limits of contemporary, usually Western, culture.

Desacralisation

This form of the secularisation process is concerned with the increasing 'matter-of-factness' of modern society. It assumes that no special esoteric-supernatural forces operate within the world, and that life can be lived in accordance with human rationality. Schneider (1970:176) sums up the end result of this process as a world where 'Entities of the type of spirits and leprechauns are more and more removed from the field of what men think they witness when they look around them'. Shiner (1967) suggests that it is a world 'gradually deprived of its sacred character', where the phenomena of the supernatural and elements of mystery play no part.

Early sociological theorists tended to fit this general process into their evolutionary schemas. Thus Comte, a rational thinker basing his knowledge of the world solely upon empirical observation of sense data (and hence severely limiting the scope of his analysis) sought to show that this method, positivism, was the only 'true' religion – a logical, natural outcome of the evolution of man's thinking. His famous Law of the Three Stages states:

> Seen in its full completeness the fundamental law of Intellectual Evolution consists of the necessary passage of all human theories through three successive stages: first the Theological, or Fictitious, which is provisional; secondly the Metaphysical or Abstract which is transitional; and thirdly, the Positive or Scientific, which alone is definitive (Comte, 1876: 23ff).

The Metaphysical stage, effecting a transition between two 'incompatible systems' conceives of causes, not as supernatural beings (as found in the Theological stage) but as abstract forces inherent in all things. The fictitious synthesis, which relates causes to the destiny of men, acts to give mankind the requisite energy and perseverance to come to terms with industrial progress. The Metaphysical spirit is the essential agent of transition (see also Madge, 1964) therefore the agent of secularisation.

Max Weber was also concerned with irreversible process of rationalisation which was leading to a specifically disenchanted world view. Basing his analysis on the move away from the original practical and calculating rationalism of magic, through the concept of prophecy, Weber noted that the 'goal of religious behaviour is successively irrationalised until finally other-worldly non-economic goals come to represent what is distinctive in religious behaviour'. Weber also notes that two forms of prophecy are available during this transition: ethical prophecy, demanding obedience as an ethical duty to an external God; and exemplary prophecy, in which personal example leads to salvation. Each prophetic community realised its religious interests either by attempting to master or control the world as a result of directions from a god or gods (asceticism), or by devaluing or ignoring it (mysticism) (Weber, 1968 : 541ff). Each form of realisation may be divided into sub-types: world-rejecting or inner-worldly. The motivating ethic of ascetic religion is value rationality while that of mysticism is instrumental rationality. Modern society is characterised by instrumental rationality emancipated from its religious heritage and the process of emancipation being a result of ascetic religion.

Weber suggests this point, towards the end of his essay on the Protestant Ethic, as a possible field for further investigation. 'Modern man is in general, even with the best will, unable to give religious ideas a significance for culture and national character which they deserve', he says, having noted the significance of ascetic rationalism. Since further investigation would relate ascetic rationalism to social ethics, organisational types, cultural elements, philosophy and science, the historical development from medieval beginnings to utilitarian dissolution could be traced so that 'the quantitative cultural influence of ascetic Protestantism in relation to other plastic elements of modern culture be estimated' (Weber, 1958:182ff).

In his essay, 'Science as a Vocation', Weber notes that modern society is

Characterised by rationalisation and intellectualisation and, above all, by the 'disenchantment of the world'. Precisely the ultimate and most sublime values have retreated from public life either in the transcendental realm of mystic life or into the brotherliness of direct and personal human relations (Gerth and Mills, 1968:155).

Weber explains that intellectualisation and rationalisation are not related to increased knowledge about the world, only to a different way of regarding it.

It means that principally there are no mysterious incalculable forces that come into play, but rather that one can in principle, master all things by calculation.

R. N. Nisbet describes this form of secularisation, one of the four major processes of historical change (with individuation, innovation and politicisation) as:

that in which the dominance of religious or sacred values in a population is terminated, however briefly, among however small a minority of the population, by values drawn directly from human reason (Nisbet, 1970:387).

He argues that Weber's conception of rationalisation as the underlying basis for change has specific political and organisational connotations, and proposes a broader understanding of Weber's analysis.

The process of secularisation results in the novel respect for values of utility rather than of sacredness alone, control of the enviroment rather than passive submission to it, and, in some ways most importantly, concern with man's present welfare on this earth rather than his supposed immortal relations to the Gods (Nisbet, 1970:383).

Nisbet also notes that Weber was not really concerned to show rationalisation, or secularisation, to be an inexorable process through which all societies must pass, but rather that it could occur at different times and in different places. His great feat however, was

to be able to show the connection between . . . secularisation or rationalisation and such dissimilar forms of behaviour and thought as the structure of the modern state, the entrepreneurial system in the economy, the rise of the European style of military organisation, and modern science, as well as certain distinctive forms of art, philosophy and music.

Nisbet also discusses the identification between the rise of modern technology and the process of disenchantment.

Technology may be described as the institutionalization of utilitarian norms. It is the largest category within which all norms of utility, convenience, efficiency, organization and human reason may be placed (Nisbet, 1970:244–5).

Technology has become applied not only to space and matter, but also to human beings themselves. 'Technology replaces enchantment.' This is an ongoing process at the present time, but it is not exclusive, since technology can also breed an anti-technical form of irrationality, with its concomitant 'revolt' against modernism.[14] Shiner notes that:

The inherent problem with the desacralization view is its assumption that religion is intrinsically bound up with an understanding of the world as permeated by sacred powers (1967:216).

He goes on to point out that Judaeo-Christianity is a religious tradition which desacralises itself, and that, as a result, this thesis can only be applied to societies within that tradition with some qualifications. Mary Douglas (1970) has attempted to show that the necessary modernity which seems to attend many of the manifestations of this thesis (specifically in relation to modern science and technology) is misplaced because it implies that primitive man is by nature deeply religious. She dimisses this as nonsense. The truth is that all the varieties of scepticism, materialism and spiritual fervour are to be found in the range of tribal societies. At least Weber in 'Science as a Vocation' realised that the obverse, the complete rational scepticism of modern man, was also perhaps, an oversimplification, when he warns that, 'the methods of science cannot enlighten us about the *meaning* of the world'.

Secularism

The doctrine of secularism has its origins in the late nineteenth century, most especially in the works of its first great proponent C. J. Holyoake. He defined it as:

> a code of duty pertaining to this life, founded on considerations purely human, and intended mainly for those who find theology indefinite, or inadequate, unreliable and unbelievable (1896:41).

However, he distinguishes between the doctrines of secularism and the concept of the secular instruction which

> is far more limited in its range than Secularisation, which defends secular pursuits against theology, where theology attacks them or obstructs them. But pure secular knowledge is confined to its own pursuit . . . (1896:62).

Hence secularism denies the existence of a sacred order and approximates more to intellectual agnosticism.

It is thus different from the earlier concept of secularity, which is identified, for example, by N. Berkes as

> The conflict between the forces of tradition which tend to promote the domination of religion and sacred law, and the force of change (1964:6).

He specifically notes that secularism and secularity are different elements, and each is possible within the same society. He proposes, however, to use the word secularism as a wider concept in order to make it usable within the Moslem context, and hence his change in the meaning of the term to that covered by the present use of 'secularity'.

Groethuysen defines secularism as 'the attempt to establish an autonomous sphere of knowledge purged of supernatural, fideistic presuppositions' (1934:651). The distinction which allowed scholars to differentiate between faith and knowledge, while not denying revealed theology its existence, resulted in a 'philosophical, or natural, theology, which placed its chief emphasis on the truth perceptible by the human reason'. His analysis of the development

46

of the necessary cultural environment for the growth c
is part of the disestablishment thesis, with the vital impe
ing from the Reformation.

This view is very similar to the French concept of l
(Bosworth, 1962) which contains a whole philosophical
based on a view of society and humanity expressly denyi
existence of a religious underpinning. Dansette (quoted by ̨os-
worth) sees it as 'the negator of Catholicism and the propagator
of a rationalist religion which puts man in the place of God'. However, the discussion of church–state relations in France is also very
mixed up with the earlier concept of disengagement and laicité.

Nierman (1970) quotes the Archbishop of Cambrai as describing the difference between 'laicité' and 'laicisme' as the difference
between religious neutrality, where the state is 'neither for nor
against religion', and an anti-religious ideology based on 'agnostic
materialism or an ideological atheism'. In the French case, secularism arose from the outcome of the Enlightenment and the French
Revolution.

St-Simon and Comte provided the 'new religion' of humanity
during the nineteenth century. Society would be organised on a
rational basis with the Gospel put into practice on a large scale
for the first time. One such system was Marxist-Leninism, which
according to H. J. Blackham, is 'sustained by metaphysical ideas
and utopian ideals' (1966:46). He suggests that, not only was
Christianity laicised into socialism, but it was laicised into nationalism via Hegel's 'scientific socialism'. The modern forms are Existentialism and Humanism, but it is also possible to suggest that contemporary religious humanism might also fall into this category.[15]

A more specific view of the doctrine of secularity, which is also
more obviously a theory of secularisation, is provided by Guy
Swanson (1968). He follows through the analyses of O'Dea, Bellah,
and Cox's *The Secular City*, to conclude that the identifiable elements revolve around man's relationship with God.

> For Calvin, man's secular activity was undertaken for the
> greater glory of God. For Cox, the modern Protestant's secular
> activity is a share with God in a common task (1968:817).

But, as the result of generic forms of the secularisation process, the
gradual differentiation of religious values to provide a broad over-
arching umbrella, all participants in life become subordinated (using
Simmel's phrase) to the exigencies of a common principle. Hence
it is only the specific situational requirements which can justify any
hierarchical organisation.

Swanson's analysis leads him to define 'modern secularity' (in

47

terms of this analysis, modern secularism) by suggesting that

> The newest phases of social evolution enable and impel the clarification – in terms of 'corporate actor' – of the very core of the society's normative character, of the society's very 'identity', if you will; and a man as an individual person relates to that 'identity' of his society as to a collective person; and all participants in the society are equal by virtue of the depth of their dependence on others for nurture as persons (1968 : 827).

However, he sees no evidence of an upward trend in secularism in America. He quotes several studies from America and other countries, but admits their frailties, particularly the tendency to investigate the more 'authentic' forms of secularism noted above.

Perhaps the most fundamental limitation of this form of secularisation is the ideological nature of secularism itself. As a result, the problem of the functional similarity between a secular movement, such as Humanism, and the religion of which it is a secularised form, occurs (Robertson, 1970 : 39). Its solution, in terms of conventionally defined religion, lays it open to the process of mythification.

There is an attendant problem of identifying the exact meaning of secularism as an anti-religious ideology. This relates, to some extent, to the difficulty of adequately identifying relevant tendencies in contemporary society. Thus Schneider refers to high levels and low levels of belief – something which can be translated easily to unbelief.

Charles Glock (1971), following most contemporary sociologists (Caporale and Grumelli, 1971; Budd, 1973 are examples), suggests that organisations whose members fail to experience the sacred, or feel subject to its authority, are best labelled as having 'unbelief'. He develops a fourfold classification based upon the dichotomous pairs of subjectivist/objectivist authority, and its natural/supernatural reference. These are summarised in Table 2.2.

TABLE 2.2

	Supernatural referent	*Natural referent*
Objectivist authority	Organised religion	Political/social creed, e.g., Communism
Subjectivist authority	Existential religion	Secular movement, e.g., Humanism

Source: Glock (1971:56–7).

He then notes that unbelief can have a variety of meanings depending upon which particular viewpoint within the classification forms its basis:

> Logically, the system allows for only one definition of unbelief – namely, the failure to score as a believer in any of the four belief categories. Unbelief may also be defined, however, from the perspective of each belief category; thus, one may speak of objectivist – supernatural believers and unbelievers. ... Additional definitions of unbelief may stem from a narrower conception of objectivist belief. Thus from the perspective of Christian belief, a non-Christian would be an unbeliever . . . (Glock, 1971:57).

Hence it would seem that the notion of unbelief, at least, is best understood as having a specific religious referent, and is thus essentially a negative definition.

This forms the basis for Campbell's objections to the traditional sociological approach. He feels that a more descriptive, and also more accurate term than unbelief is irreligion, since it can refer to all aspects including action, attitude and experience (Campbell, 1971:63). Irreligion is a unique feature of contemporary society, but unbelief has probably always been present in some form:

> the role which irreligion occupies in contemporary societies is a distinctive feature of these societies . . . in the existence of irreligion, both organised and unorganised, manifesting itself to some extent in all social strata and having a degree of social and legal recognition, modern societies appear to be unique (Campbell, 1971:5).

This leads Campbell to suggest that the development of irreligious organisations can be used as an index of the secularism process. He states:

> The fact the irreligious movements act as agents of secularisation has strangely been overlooked by sociologists. ... In the cultural context they act as propagators of a rational scientific world view. . . . Alternatively, irreligion in its organised or unorganised form can be taken as evidence of secularisation and the growth of irreligious movements treated on data indicating the decline of religion . . . (Campbell, 1971:7).

Conclusion

The social myth of a secularisation process is well illustrated in

49

the discussions above, which are based on definitions of religion which are primarily normative in origin. The fundamental premise, in all four cases, seems to be that contemporary society, and more often, contemporary American society, is the best example of a truly secular society.

Each individual analysis either limits itself specifically to the USA (e.g. Bellah, Parsons, Herberg, Swanson) or to a specific historical period (e.g. Weber, Troeltsch, Bosworth), but is then happily generalised to a broad conception of secularisation without any recognition of the ideological limitations which govern the outcome of the discussion.

In the case of secularisation seen as a generalisation of religion into an over-arching normative order, methodological problems also intrude in such a way as to make most of the analyses meaningless, except as descriptive of unique circumstances in the development of American pluralism.

Such discussions would appear to be quite irrelevant, as Bellah himself notes (in the cases of Japan and Turkey), to the process of secularisation in other countries. All such analyses seem to be based implicitly upon the notion of desacralisation current in the late nineteenth century. These can be summarised as an inevitable *progression* of society, often towards bigger, better and less religious things.

Hence these forms of secularisation are rooted in a particularly potent 'ideology of progress', which has raised them to the level of social myths.

(c) Cognitively based

The final section explicating the substantive aspect of discussion of the secularisation process is primarily concentrated on two kinds of process: segmentation, and secularisation itself. I have left the use of this term until Category III – the category in which the definition of religion tends to be cognitive – because it describes a fairly coherent, specifically sociological, tradition. Hence, if a sociological use of the term secularisation *could* be readily identified it would stem most probably from this final category. The latter part of the following analysis will be concerned with some of the underlying 'logics' which often appear to be confused with the secularisation process.

Segmentation

This discussion of the secularisation process owes much to recent development in phenomenological sociology as elaborated by Berger and Luckmann.[16] Their primary concern is with explaining how religion and religious institutions develop, and their analysis of the process of secularisation stems directly from this concern. Luckmann provided the initial impetus for this discussion in his famous critique of church oriented religion: *The Invisible Religion* (1967).

The individual becomes human – that is, achieves a self-concept – by embarking with others on a social construction of reality. Luckmann identifies this 'transcendence of biological nature' as a religious phenomenon and accepts that the logical outcome of this view is that religion is an 'all encompassing phenomenon'. His reply to criticism on this score is that social analysis does no more than 'identify general sources from which spring the historically differentiated social forms of religion. This moral universe becomes completely internalised'.

Some aspects of life are not, however, concrete and unproblematic, and fit uneasily into the wholly internalised world view. They are not amenable to habitual response. Such areas, says Luckmann (1967: 59ff), are experienced as 'different' and 'mysterious', and the two domains tend to become polarised, though 'necessarily apprehended as being related in some manner'. Language, along with ritual action and sacred things, provides the necessary articulation of this sacred cosmos through its symbolic potential.

> The symbols which represent the reality of the sacred cosmos may be termed religious representations because they perform, in a specific and concentrated way, the broad religious function of the world view as a whole. The world view in its totality was defined earlier as a universal and unspecific form of religion. Consequently, the configuration of religious representations that form a *sacred universe* is to be defined *as a specific historical social form of religion* (1967: 61).

Because the sacred cosmos is part of the world view, it forms part of the objective social reality and does not necessarily become institutionally manifest. It determines the socialisation process of the individual, and hence religious representations 'serve to legitimate conduct in the full range of social institutions'.

However, Luckmann notes that this is likely to occur only in relatively simple society – that is, one with a low degree of institutional differentiation and a 'relatively homogeneous social distribution of the world view'. In such a society, no institutional basis for the specifically religious representations is manifested. The establishment of specialised religious institutions results from the articulation of the sacred cosmos in the world view. This provides the necessary, but not the sufficient condition which is met through the structural differentiation of social roles through the division of labour. Only by producing surplus manpower can fully specialised religious roles and religious experts be achieved.

In an increasingly heterogeneous society, laymen participate less and less directly in the sacred cosmos, and rely increasingly on the 'mediation of experts' in their relationships to it. Luckmann concludes:

> If religiously relevant conduct originally rests on fully internalised norms and general social controls, conformity in such matters is increasingly supervised by religious specialists in 'complex' societies. While religious representation originally serves to legitimate conduct in all kinds of situations, increasing the specialisation of religion results in the transfer of social control over 'religious behaviour' to specific institutions. The vested interest of the religious experts in the recruitment and training of their successors, in the exclusion of laymen from the 'higher' forms of sacred knowledge and in defence of privileges against competing for these experts, typically relate to the formation of some kind of 'ecclesiastic' organisation (1967: 66).

The concrete historical person is usually born into an already existing society and world view, which becomes an objective and stable social fact. The process of socialisation transforms this objective fact into subjective reality. The two, that is the objective official world view and subjective reality, can correspond identically only in the simplest (and hence hypothetical) form of society. This ideal type has no institutional, organised religious forms, and implies a complete identity between the church, the sacred cosmos and the hierarchy of meaning in the world view. It also assumes perfect socialisation.

Luckmann suggests that in relatively simple societies, 'individuals typically internalise most of a relatively homogeneous culture'. In more complex societies this difficulty cannot be overlooked since it is precisely in such societies that institutionalised specialisation occurs. There can be no high degree of congruence between the 'official' model of religion and the subjective system of 'ultimate significance'.

The other end of the continuum is also not logically tenable. It describes a society where the official models of religion and the individual system of ultimate significance are wholly incongruent, that is, where no member of the society is socialised into the official model. In this case, such a model would cease to be official. But Luckmann suggests an alternative view, namely the replacement of one 'official' model by another, perhaps on a generational basis. Hence Luckmann's view of the secularisation process is concerned with the *relative* congruence between the two factors.

In conclusion, Luckmann describes the history of Western civilisation in terms of this continuum, with a return to almost complete congruence during the Middle Ages after the breakdown of the Roman Empire. However, the process of rapid social change which has come to characterise modern industrial society has had its effect on the development of the church.

She gained a high degree of internal autonomy and her institutional structure was characterised by the trend to functional rationality. The validity of her norms became restricted to a specifically 'religious sphere', while the global claims of the 'official' model were generally neutralised as mere rhetoric (Luckmann, 1967:95).

The social-psychological correlate of institutional segmentation is seen by Luckmann as the segregation of 'rational' institutional norms in the consciousness of the individual. The breakdown of an 'overarching biographical context of significance' results in the emergence of the 'private sphere' with an illusory sense of individual autonomy. This in turn results in a relative freedom to construct a personal identity, and hence the development of a consumer orientation. Luckmann therefore suggests that:

'Secularisation' in its early phases was not a process in which traditional sacred values simply faded away. It was a process in which autonomous institutional 'ideologies' replaced, within their own domain, an overarching and transcendent universe of norms (1967:107).

These two are not identical, however, because the newly constructed system of private 'ultimate significance' is based on the selection of 'certain religious themes from the available assortment', and not on the 'diffusion of the sacred cosmos through the institutional structure of society or through institutional specialisation of religion' (Berger and Luckmann, 1966). Such themes are also to be found distributed through a large variety of secondary institutions including *Playboy* and the *Readers' Digest*.

Berger operates with a much narrower definition of religion than Luckmann. He states, in an appendix:

I question the utility of a definition that equates religion with the human *tout court*. It is one thing to point up the anthropological foundation of religion in the human capacity for self-transcendence, quite another to equate the two. There are, after all, modes of self transcendence and concomitant symbolic universes that are vastly different from each other, whatever the identity of the anthropological origins (1969a : 178).

The identification of a humanly meaningful world, therefore, need not be sacred for Berger, Religious activity serves as a reminder of the reality maintaining force of religious ideation, but 'worlds are socially constructed and socially maintained' and these worlds require a 'social base' that is real to actual human beings. This base may be called the plausibility structure. Hence the reality of the socially constructed religious world requires a social structure within which its reality is taken for granted.

When the plausibility structure is strong, there is little need to develop the complex legitimations which generally occur when it is threatened. The major variable lies in the scope of the plausibility structure. The problem of world maintenance is greater when the plausibility structure for the religious world is served only by part of the social structure.

Through the increasing differentiation of society and its concomitant increase in the division of labour, plausibility structures no longer encompass the whole social structure. The process of secularisation has removed sectors of society from this dominance by religious institutions or symbols (Berger, 1969a : 107ff). The diversity of social roles in modern industrial society allows for a multiplicity of possible plausibility structures. They cannot disappear because of the threat of anomie, and the problem of theodicy is to maintain their validity.

Modern society is also characterised by structural rationalisation which is institutionally manifested in the phenomenon of bureaucracy. The result for religious institutions is that, 'irrespective of their various theological traditions', they appear increasingly similar in structure. This process of bureaucratisation occurs both in their internal and their external social relations, and increasingly, religious groups see the clergy as 'personnel', conversion or attendance as 'results', the laity as customers, and different religious groups as fellow organisations with similar problems (Berger, 1969a : 138ff).

Berger notes that, as long as religious institutions held a monopolistic position in the social structure, they could control the plausibility content of their theology. But:

The pluralistic situation . . . introduces a novel form of mundane influences, probably more potent in modifying religious contents than such older forms as the wishes of kings or the vested interest of classes – the dynamics of consumer preference. To repeat, the crucial sociological and social-psychological characteristic of the pluralist situation is that religion can no longer be imposed but must be marketed (1969a : 144).

In this, Berger reaches much the same conclusion as Luckmann, but he side-steps the difficulty he sees in Luckmann's conflation of non-specific, elementary social forms of religion and specific historical social forms. This leads him (especially in *A Rumour of Angels*, 1969b) to promote a view of the market situation as one of competing plausibility structures *within* the originally defined religious world view. Thus elements of Buddhism may compete with Mohammedanism, which in turn may compete with elements of Christianity, but science or Communism remain on the level of functional alternatives outside this particular market situation. Berger concludes:

It is safe to predict that the future of religions everywhere will be decisively shaped by the forces that have been discussed in this and preceeding chapters – secularisation, pluralisation, and 'subjectivisation' – and by the manner in which the several religious institutions will react to these (1969a : 171).

Two major drawbacks limit the theoretical usefulness of this analysis. First, there is no way of isolating the degree of malintegration necessary to produce radical departures from the 'taken-for-granted' viewpoints, since presumably all societies produce *some* areas of marginality. To suggest, as Berger seems to, that this problem is overcome by postulating a process of 'continuous socialisation' seems to bypass the problem. Either the objective view of reality no longer fits the internal view, or it continues to do so through a gradual process of change. Both cases require similar means of adjustment, though on different scales. In either case, since we do not know beforehand what constitutes the 'critical level', this sort of analysis can be applied only retrospectively.

The second drawback involves the direction taken by such changes as may occur. Berger traces the routes of the secularisation process to the demythologisation arising from Old Testament Judaism. He does not link this historical discourse with the earlier discussion of social change, so that no satisfactory explanation is given of why such a demythologising tradition should arise. Furthermore, Berger offers no systematic discussion of the relation between ancient magical or mystical religion, and the specific religious culture which he labels secularised.[17] Like Bellah, he too is limited to accepting social history as a substitute for sociological theory.

Turning to his conclusion, much of what Berger has to say about the market element of modern society is foreshadowed by Tönnies' famous work *Gemeinschaft und Gesellschaft* (1955). In this, Tönnies suggests that all the major institutions in society, and also the personal relationships, are moving towards a *Gesellschaft* characterisation. However, as Berger himself points out, such a situation involves a concept of 'ecstacy', of being able to stand outside the 'taken-for-granted' routines of daily life. In other words it involves complete freedom of choice. The logical outcome of this freedom, with its implied loss of structural underpinning, is either the creation of novel structures, or total anomie. This is a problem Berger shrinks from confronting by accepting the theodicies of existing forms of religious symbolism as the basis for choice. Hence his final analysis stops short of secularisation within his own definition of the term.

Secularisation

Perhaps the most overworked distinction within the sociology of religion is the one which separates the sacred from the secular or profane. Movements along this continuum are most often seen as evidence of the process of secularisation. The index for identifying such moves varies with the theorist involved, but one of the first was suggested by Tönnies (1955).

The continuum postulated by Tönnies has *Gemeinschaft* (community) and *Gesellschaft* (association) as its two polar types. The former is based on the Natural Will, which is 'immanent in activity', while the latter is based on the Rational Will which is 'prior to the activity to which it occurs . . .'. Concord, based on communal understanding of motives, represents the most elementary form of *Gemeinschaft*, though the concept is not directly related to scale. Concord functions to provide group solidarity, binding society through common customs and beliefs.

Religion (Tönnies, 1955: 71ff) in such circumstances is fundamentally ritualistic, based on tradition, and related to maintaining feelings of communality and harmony. It is instinctive, emotional, all-embracing and unquestioned, relating the individual to his social group by providing solid and unquestionable answers to the problems encountered in marginal situations. It provides the basis for deciding moral questions and validates customary patterns of behaviour. In no way can it be regarded as providing a legitimation for a questioning outlook on life.

The concept of *Gesellschaft* is essentially negative. It is based on rationality and forethought, and actions performed in *Gesellschaft* society tend to be individually rather than communally inspired. The basis is not concord but contract.

The contract is the result of two divergent individual wills, intersecting at one point. The contract lasts until the exchange has been completed, and it wills and demands the execution of the two acts of which it consists (Tönnies, 1955 : 82).

Relationships become impersonal and secondary, and the individual regards them as specific and unique, to be entered into only when it is in his interest to do so. Action becomes more conventional than customary.

The concept of contract is opposed to family law (following Sir Henry Maine's seminal *Ancient Law*) which is rooted in the concept of 'status'. Status is to be found therefore in the realm of *Gemeinschaft*. The move from *Gemeinschaft* to *Gesellschaft* is not direct, but in either case a common unity of will is necessary to keep society together. In the case of *Gemeinschaft* this is provided by faith, for the individual, and by religion, for the society as a whole. The parallels for *Gesellschaft* are theory and public opinion.

Thus religion assumes authority over commonwealth, public opinion over state. Religion approves folkways, mores and customs as good and right or condemns them as false or bad. Likewise public opinion condemns policy and legislation as effective and clever, or condemns it as ineffective and stupid (Tönnies, 1955 : 283).

In *Gesellschaft* society, religion becomes impossible because the relationships which religion sustained are no longer present (the binding of the group, the common heritage, etc.) A common heritage and belief would be a hindrance in this situation since the individual becomes responsible for his own fate. He is more concerned with the contractual relationship to the state. Hence Tönnies views the secularisation process as an inevitable by-product of the move from *Gemeinschaft* to *Gesellschaft*. The impetus for this change lies in rationality, which involves forethought. Religion, based on faith, will only be significant in a society based on concord, where action is instinctive. The process of secularisation is more a change of emphasis, since Tönnies was only concerned to isolate *predominant* variables within a society, rather than a distinct institutional transformation.

Durkheim (1915) operated with a much broader definition of religion than Tönnies, and his analysis of the effects of the division

57

E

of labour on social organisation did not envisage the disappearance of religion, but rather that it would change in its outward forms. 'Religion is something eminently social. Religious representations are collective representations which express collective realities . . .' (1915:10).

Utilising several ideas common in his day (including those of Tönnies), Durkheim set out two polar types of social solidarity: mechanical and organic. On the one hand, social relationships are face-to-face and social control is vested in the group which can be identified as society; on the other, relationships are secondary, with social control stemming from the complex inter-relationships of groups within society. Nevertheless, religion is an integral part of both. In the former, society is the group which celebrates its collectivity in the religious act. In the latter, the various groups within society are seen as celebrating, not only their internal affinity, but also their affinity with the society at large. No man is a religious island.[18]

Durkheim does not only distinguish the forms of the division of labour found in mechanical and organic forms of social solidarity, but also isolates a possible transitional stage which he describes as exhibiting abnormal or pathological forms of the division of labour (Durkheim, 1933, bk III). This seems to represent the 'secularising' element in Durkheim's analysis.

The 'anomic' division of labour is Durkheim's description of the class of events which stem from a breakdown of social solidarity with the increasing division of labour. He takes as his example the economic market. Here, the segmentation of life leads to a small number of markets with limited scope. The producers are near enough to the consumers to ensure an equilibrium, but there is a possibility that eventually some markets will grow by fusing with others, and the necessary expansion in production can grow to super-national dimensions. The producer is then no longer sufficiently in touch with the consumers to maintain equilibrium, and accordingly production becomes unbridled and unregulated. In personal terms, if the worker can continue to work only through routine because he does not know what end of his work proceeds, 'he is no longer anything but an inert piece of machinery'.

This contradiction is not, according to Durkheim, inherent in the division of labour, but is the result of exceptional and abnormal circumstances. These can also result in the 'forced division of labour' where the discrepancy between the distribution of functions and the distribution of talents results in class warfare, etc. Using his biological analogy, each cell fulfils its functions and feels no need to usurp the functions of other cells, an ideal impossible in human society because of the intrusion of the human element.

Religion, in a society dominated by pathological forms of the division of labour, atrophies. 'Men cannot celebrate ceremonies for which they see no reason, nor can they accept a faith which they in no way understand' (Durkheim, 1915:430). Hence religion in the particular sense founders in the face of societal contradiction, even though the recognition of the 'sacred' will always remain. The secularisation process is linked directly to the development of these contradictions, but it is a temporary (though not necessarily short-lived) phenomenon which precedes the advent of the ideal organic forms of social solidarity.

Robert Redfield (1947) and Howard Becker (1950) are only two of the many students who have extended the basic conceptualisations developed by Tönnies and Durkheim.[19] Redfield's folk–urban continuum is based on empirical observation of primitive and urbanised society. The former is generally small, isolated and homogeneous, with conventionalised forms of living in which behaviour is traditional, spontaneous and personal. There is no reflection for intellectual ends; the sacred prevails over the secular. Urbanised society fulfils the opposite criteria. However, Redfield (quoting Sol Tax), is not at all certain that the sacred element in society is identical with 'a stable society . . . small, unsophisticated and homogeneous in beliefs'. He concludes:

> It may appear that under certain conditions a literate, and indeed, at least partly urbanised society may be both highly commercial and sacred . . . while under certain other conditions an otherwise folklike people may become individualistic, commercial and perhaps secular (1947: 308).

Howard Becker is more certain of the gradual disappearance of the sacred.[20] He defines the sacred as including such concepts as the holy, spiritual, godly and the religious. However, the central aspect is the respected, venerated and above all inviolable, position of a tradition. A sacred society is one which renders its members unwilling or unable, in whatever measure, to accept the new.

> Otherwise put, a network of sociation that develops, among the personalities weaving and woven by it, a high degree of resistance to change, particularly in their social order, is a sacred society. A secular society is one that elicits or imparts to its members, by means of sociation, willingness and ability to respond to the culturally new as the new is defined by these members in terms of the society's existing culture (1950: 352-3).

The continuum is seen therefore as a scale ranging from maximum readiness to change. Becker uses the criterion of the sacrifice of life on behalf of both types of extreme situation (prevention or pursuit of change) as an indicator, and in addition utilises the situational criteria of isolation and accessibility. He concludes with four constructed types of society – proverbial, prescriptive, principal, pro-normless but notes that empirically a great deal of inter-mixing can occur. No society is seen as all of one piece. Change is not necessarily evolutionary, nor even developmental, and Becker suggests that extreme sacredness has sometimes been transmuted into its direct opposite, extreme secularisation (see also Berkes, 1964; Bellah, 1958).

The opposition between the sacred and the profane or secular has been subject to very strong criticism both on the grounds that it does not provide a continuum, and also that it is not a polarity. David Martin (1969b, chapter 1) for example, discusses one possible meaning of sacred (other-worldliness) and shows succinctly that two problems are concerned – the linking of a variety of polar types into various continua, and the selection of one crucial dichotomy to illustrate the required content. Another point of criticism concerns the direction of the move along any continua or between polar types, which is invariably away from the sacred end. The similarity between the non-sacred form and contemporary society cannot be overlooked, with its attendant possibility of ideological preconception affecting the analyses. This appears to intrude through the use of Western, industrial social structure at one end of the continua.

Three underpinning 'logics'

The process of secularisation has been seen also as part of three related master-trends of social change: urbanisation, industrialisation and modernisation. In a way, they provide the underlying 'logic' in most of the analyses discussed above, although they can be seen as more obviously linked to the last, based upon the notion of continua between ideal societal types.

The 'logic' involved in any particular example is difficult to isolate given the nature of the inter-relationships between the three processes. Analytically, however, any one of the master trends can be used as a starting point.

In the case of urbanisation, the move away from a rural setting implies changes in life-styles which are closely related to the industrialisation process, and which could be subsumed under the general rubric of modernisation. The old rural values, social controls, and way of life are necessarily destroyed and replaced by new values and a highly accelerated life-style. Concomitantly, there is a disruption of social ties and an increasing rise in social isolation, as well as a decreasing reliance on the ever shrinking, stable and durable, aspects of social life. As Yinger notes when discussing the modernisation of America:

> Commerce, industrial specialisation, the development of larger and longer factories with their costly machine-tools and equipment, and rapid urbanisation – these and other changes were forming the reorganisation of the lives of ever-increasing numbers of people. The relatively self-sufficient and independent farmer and handicraftsman lost control of the tools with which they worked and the skills which had given them some independence. In large numbers they were becoming unskilled and semi-skilled factory workers. The whole society became vastly independent, creating moral problems that were unknown to stable, agricultural societies (1957:220).

By implication, traditional forms of religion necessarily change as a result of this 'logic' which treats religion as a dependent variable. Such a view has a relatively long pedigree which can be traced to the work of Marx and Engels (1964) with their emphasis on the primacy of the material-economic base as the instigator of social change.

The primacy of the economic structure is considered important, in a slightly different way, by Simmel in his discussion of 'Metropolis and Mental Life' (1950) where he considers the effects of a money economy upon the nature of social relationships in an urban setting. His discussion leads him to suggest that an individual's outlook is transformed completely, and that all his social relationships are affected, including religious ones. This forces him to a more secular (defined as non-traditional) viewpoint. He concludes that individualism is the hallmark of metropolitan life, and that it results either in individual independence (and existential religion), or in an elaboration of individuality itself.

Harvey Cox (1968, chapter 2ff) comes to a similar conclusion from another direction when he emphasises the anonymity and mobility which characterise urban living. However, his conclusion regarding secularisation assumes a continuity between pre-urban and urban religion through a reinterpretation of the Bible:

> There is no reason why Christians should deplore the accelerating mobility of the modern metropolis. The Bible does not call man to renounce mobility, but to 'go to a place that I will show unto you'. . . . High mobility is no assurance of salvation, but neither is it an obstacle to faith (Cox, 1968:71).

61

The 'logic' of industrialism shifts the emphasis towards the primacy of technological advances and its effects on work and communications. Berger, supposedly analysing a dialectical relationship between religion and society, says:

A modern, industrial society requires the presence of large cadres of scientific and technical personnel, whose training and ongoing organisation presupposes a high degree of rationalisation, not only on the level of infra-structure but also on that of consciousness. Any attempts at traditionalistic reconquista thus threatens to dismantle the rational foundations of modern society. Furthermore, the secularising potency of capitalistic-industrial rationalisation is not only self-perpetuating but self-aggrandizing (1969a : 131).

Scotford-Archer and Vaughan (1970) analysing Berger's 'logic', suggest that industrialisation appears to have resulted in 'structural imperatives of production' which make secularisation inevitable. However, they point out that, historically, this would be an inaccurate analysis because of the various exceptions which can be found. They also note that Berger extends his thesis to a worldwide perspective, suggesting that westernisation and modernisation have resulted in global secularisation.

Modernisation, then, provides the third 'logic' underlying secularisation theories. It describes a process whereby the values and the structure of contemporary industrial society are improved (in some way) relative to societies which are still primarily traditional-rural in character.[21] This process is part of a more general theory of development, and describes a continuum between traditional and modern societal models. Bellah, in assessing the important cognitive changes which occur in this process, translates them to the level of the social system, and concludes:

Progress thus involves not merely learning but also learning capacity, and increasing ability to 'learn to learn'. This kind of learning capacity includes the 'capacity for deep arrangements of inner structure, and thus for the development of radically new functions' (1965 : 169–70).

The result is a breakdown of traditional religious forms in societies which have become successfully modernised (see Yinger 1971, chapter 17).

Perhaps the most serious criticism of the underlying 'logics' of urbanisation, industrialisation and modernisation centres on the validity of the suggested necessary sequence of cause and effect. Scotford-Archer and Vaughan, for example, suggest that the accompanying process of de-secularisation, or even of re-secularisation, which is a point also made by Nisbet (1970:388). Certainly, their conclusions that insufficient evidence has been provided, lends greater credence to the notion that the processes discussed are, in reality, no more than trends, and that their relationships to the process of secularisation are unclear.

Conclusion

Once more the secularisation process, as outlined by analyses based on definitions of religion which have both institutional and normative referents, appears to have attained mythical status.

The two major analyses discussed appear to have extended their boundaries to attain global significance in ways which well illustrate Toulmin's criteria for recognising the presence of social myths. Much of the blame for this can be seen to rest with the 'logics' which underpin most views of secularisation, and which are most prevalent in the processes classified in this third category.

Thus segmentation and, more importantly, 'secularisation' (as outlined above) rest on the assumption of an inner dynamic which represents the secularising fever. Critics have noted that some of these 'logics' are irrelevant since they could equally well justify re-secularisation. Others have noted that the usage appears stretched beyond the limitation, often contemporary Western society, imposed upon the original analyses. Finally, the possibility of ideology intruding as a rationale for the loss of 'community', and as an explanation of the alienation of life in industrial society, is also somewhat in evidence. In a way, this mirrors the 'ideology of progress' which was isolated in the second category. Thus both segmentation and the commonly used sociological theory of secularisation can be seen to have attained the status of social myths.

(d) Conclusion

This chapter has fulfilled a variety of tasks. In the first instance it has highlighted the variety and breadth of the analyses of the secularisation process to be found in the sociological literature without even attempting to be exhaustive. Second, it has shown up their various internal limitations. Third, it has suggested a critique from the standpoint of an implicit ideology of progress.

The main thrust has been to show that conventional definitions of religion and religiosity appear to take precedence over sociological ones. This was illustrated in the wide range both of processes involved and empirical evidence in their support. The starting points for secularisation seemed either lost in the depths of antiquity, or lodged in some immediately pre-industrial epoch, or at almost any point in between. Secularisation itself then referred to the institutional manifestations of religion, or to some elements in the normative structure of society, or to some aspect of the *Weltanschauung* or way of seeing the world. In many cases the continua suggested were either simple dichotomies with polar types seen either in specifically historical or ideal–typical terms, or descriptive of some real or perceived historical trends.

The search for an understanding of the theoretical paucity of these attempts, however wide-ranging the empirical evidence or the generalisations that stemmed from it, seemed to hinge on the most significant features of nearly all the analyses: the reliance on contemporary Western industrial society as being in some way less 'religious' than the society with which comparisons were being made.

It was therefore suggested that most 'theories' of the secularisation process are really generalisations from limited empirical findings used by sociologists to bolster an implicit ideology of progress.

This chapter, therefore, combines an empirical critique with an exposition of the non-unitary nature of the concept of the secularisation process by illuminating the ideological underpinning to many of the uses involved. In addition, of course, the several processes have been subjected to their own 'internal' critique in order to highlight some of the deficiencies overlooked by their propagators. However, an empirical critique cannot provide sufficient evidence to discuss the use of a sociological concept without exploring the reasons why such empirical material cannot be transformed, through generalisation, into a theoretical model of change in religion. Hence, the next chapter will explore the main methodological reasons for criticising the secularisation processes under discussion, using Toulmin's criteria for recognising social myth-making.

3 The methodological critique

All phenomena are unique in their occurrence in space and
time – therefore no phenomena actually recur in their concrete
wholeness. In order to make these phenomena intelligible and
explicable they must be *reduced* through conceptualisation
(McKinney: 'The Process of Typification', in McKinney and
Tiryakian, 1970).

Methodology in the social sciences has been the subject of concern
for several years, reflecting the dissatisfaction felt by social scientists with the ways they approach their material, and the logic
underlying their inquiries.[1] The outcome of this concern has sometimes been confusion, which has occurred most frequently with
definitions and conceptualisations.[2] In the sociology of religion,
these problems have long been recognised, and most introductory
texts include a chapter on the range of definition and the variety
of meaning, both of religion and religiosity (Yinger, 1971; Robertson, 1970).

It was noted earlier that social myths generally have two aspects
which can be summarised as the *substantive*, relating to the ways
in which evidence is collected, and used to answer the fundamental
question involved; and *methodological*, concerned with whether
the methods used for relating the theories to empirical reality are
legitimate. Toulmin outlined several criteria by which the general
class of error upon which scientific myths are based, could be
identified. They were to serve as guidelines, and were collapsed
into three criteria, each indicating the existence of scientific myths,
either individually or together.

This chapter is concerned primarily with the methodological
aspect of social mythification. As a result the emphasis, based on
Toulmin's criteria, will be more in terms of the *approaches* to the

65

concepts, that is their underlying logic, than to the concepts themselves.

The parameters, within which these criteria are to be used, are provided by the question being asked, namely: Is contemporary society more or less religious than in the past?; i.e. has it undergone, or is it undergoing, a process of secularisation? It has already been noted that most myth-based answers rest on common-usage, or conventional definitions of the basic concepts. Conventional usage assumes that everyday conceptions of social reality have a meaning for the social scientist at a higher level than 'units of data' or 'bases for generalisation'. This distinction is clarified by Schutz, when he talks about first-order constructions and second-order constructions of reality (Schutz, 1962). McKinney uses the more descriptive labels of existential and constructed types (in McKinney and Tiryakian, 1970).

The first of each pair are 'conceptualisations by actors in the social process within social systems', while the second two of each pair stem from 'social scientists observing and exploring the social processes and systems'. Confounding these distinctions and, using McKinney's terminology, treating existential types as constructed types, constitutes the myth-making element in conventional usage.

Existential types are fundamentally 'folk-typifications' which have pre-constructed the world for the social scientist (McKinney and Tiryakin, 1970: 244). Hence concepts based entirely upon them can be characterised as pre-scientific, and of little value to the sociologist, unless taken a stage further and 'reduced through conceptualisation:

> The reduction to existential types of people in everyday life is
> for the purpose of 'living' and hence is only a start in the
> reduction process essential to the social scientist for 'knowing'
> in a more theoretical sense.

The question of secularisation rests on three assumptions whose roots appear to be found in conventional usage. These are:

(a) That there was a period when man and/or society was 'really religious'. This *idealism* of a 'base-line' society can be seen in terms of a contemporary set of 'folk-typifications', and is illustrated by the use of certain kinds of historical or anthropological data. It also assumes that religiosity can somehow be measured, and compared, on a cross-cultural basis, without much alteration to the dimensions used in contemporary society.

(b) That the impact of religion on society is uniformly distributed throughout that society. Put slightly differently, this is an assumption of religious homogeneity. The possibility that *permeation* will be affected by a whole range of intervening variables is conveniently overlooked, and often invalid generalisations are made from insufficient data and projected on to the society as a whole.

(c) That religion can be identified with the organisational and institutional forms current within contemporary society, or drawn from its history. Thus religion becomes *categorised* in terms of church, sect, or cult, with little or no recognition of the historical specificity of these concepts, nor of the complexity of analysis which surrounds them.

These three assumptions relate closely to the three altered criteria, laid down earlier, for identifying the presence of a social myth. Idealisation through the population of a 'base-line' society, or dimensions of religiosity, is open to misuse because of the necessary intervention of the investigator's own value preconceptions. This intervention is the result of the degree of 'visibility' manifested by the society, whether ancient or modern, or by the religiosity of the individual within that society. The amended criterion then becomes: Is the method being used for ideological reasons?

Permeation, with its emphasis on the religious homogeneity of society, overlooks differences and intervening variables. Often an analysis will be accurate for a specific location in time and space, but will bear no relation to reality when extended to the level of societal generalisation. In fact, a religiously homogeneous subculture may only provide a distorted picture when used to characterise the whole community. Thus, it becomes relevant to ask: Has the method become extended or distorted by additional usage, so that the conclusions no longer stem from the premises?

The error of categorisation stems from an uncritical acceptance of conventionally defined religious categories. Thus, the amended criterion for identifying the presence of a social myth becomes: Is the method used relevant to answering the specific question asked?

As has already been noted the substantively defined criteria are usually present in the range of discussions of the process of secularisation. Generally speaking, this will be necessarily true also for the methodologically defined criteria. However, there is likely to be less emphasis, in the areas analysed in the following, on the error of categorisation, particularly among those processes whose definitions of religion are rooted primarily in the normative sphere.

Idealisation

The main concerns of this chapter will be the idealisations of social scientists. These will be explored, on the one hand, with reference to a 'base-line' society for the secularisation process, and on the other, with reference to the concept of religiosity.

Robert Merton (1968:398) has argued that social structures operate with a 'functionally optimum degree of visibility' of norms and conduct, which need not coincide with complete visibility. He goes on to suggest that different social structures *require* for their effective operation, differing degrees of visibility'. He also suggests that there are certain processes within the social structure which resist full visibility:

> *Some* measure of leeway in conforming to the role expectations is pre-supposed in all groups. To have to meet the strict requirements of a role at all times, without some degree of deviation, is to experience insufficient allowances for individual differences in capacity and training and for situational exigencies which make strict conformity extremely difficult. This is one of the sources of . . . socially patterned, or even institutionalised, evasions of institutional roles (1968:397).

The sociological notion of visibility has, as its counterpart in psychology, social perception, but the mechanisms involved have yet to be theoretically clarified. However Merton does feel that, once the notion of 'visibility' is accepted, a number of important questions manifest themselves:

> Is the observability of *non*-membership groups characteristically greater with respect to their *norms and values* than with respect to the patterns of behaviour obtaining in them? Is there . . . a tendency for outsiders to develop unrealistic images of non-membership groups which, if they are positive reference groups, lead toward unqualified idealisation (or the official norms are taken at their face value) or, if they are negative reference groups, lead toward unqualified condemnation . . .? (1968:405).

Merton goes on to quote the example of a convert who becomes 'over-zealous in his conformity'. He suggests that part of the reason for this ardour may lie in a lack of 'first-hand knowledge of the nuances of allowable and patterned departures' from the established norms of the group he has just joined. He concludes that what is known of a group's attitudes, opinions, sentiments and expectations may not coincide with what that group really feels or does. Referring to decisions made by those in authority under the influence of public opinion, he says:

It is public opinion as observed not public opinion as it might in fact be, which variously affects, if it does not determine, the decisions of authorities (1968 : 407).

Merton's discussion has telling implications for the sociology of secularisation, and for the process of social myth construction. The process of secularisation involves social change, and any social change implies a base-line as well as an end-point. Generally, most theories of secularisation end with contemporary Western society, which, for the majority of sociologists involved, constitutes what Merton would describe as a membership group. However, as already noted, the starting point of these theories is generally some society in the historical past – which forms a non-membership group for the sociologist, and hence lays itself open to the kinds of misinterpretations and misrepresentations which result from their particular, functionally optimum, degree of visibility.

The process of mythification is possible under such circumstances only when the norms and values exhibited by the group are taken as identical to the actual norms and values on the basis of which the group existed. Thus David Martin's (1969b: 36) warning concerning the use, by some sociologists, of 'a Catholic utopianism which postulates a historical base-line (eleventh to thirteenth centuries?) when men were "really religious" ' becomes extremely relevant. Such a society may exist only in the minds of some sociologists and few historians. To assume that information handed down over the centuries in church records is a wholly accurate representation of what life was 'really' like during the period under discussion is to commit the methodological error of idealisation.

Merton's analysis also raises the further question of the comparability of conceptualised patterns of behaviour. Martin talks of the 'really religious', and it is assumed that what is described as 'really religious' *now*, was also 'really religious' in, for example, medieval Europe. There is little doubt that it is extremely problematic to view the notion of religiosity as a unitary concept. It becomes relevant to ask whether *dimensions* of religiosity are more useful in making cross-cultural comparisons, so that *profiles* of religiosity can be constructed. Such dimensional approaches are available in the sociology of religion, and will be explored in the last part of this chapter. However, the initial discussion will centre on the analysis of an historical base-line which is often regarded as religious, but which new evidence would suggest to be more magical.

It has been suggested that there is a major problem involving the kind of evidence which is used to establish a 'picture' of life

69

in a society, when the notion of a base-line society is used, either explicitly or implicitly, as the basis for comparison with the present day. The following discussion will be based upon two recent works which are critical of the conventional notions of the place of religion in sixteenth- and seventeenth-century England. Alan MacFarlane (1970), for example, when discussing one of the major books on the place of witchcraft during the period, says of the author: [3]

> She mistook what people *believed* to be happening for what actually *did* happen. Though she showed that people thought there was a witch-cult, she failed to demonstrate that there actually was one.

Macfarlane is concerned primarily to show the extent of witchcraft rather than its relationship to religion. As such he provides a more detailed analysis of a narrower kind than Keith Thomas (1971), whose work, in Macfarlane's words, 'offers a back-cloth . . . both complementing and expanding many of the following hypotheses.' Thomas's study analyses some of the popular beliefs of the sixteenth and seventeenth centuries, and includes, alongside religion, magic, witchcraft and astrology.

The concern with 'popular beliefs' rather than, for example, religion alone, reflects Thomas's general sociological approach to the study of history. Society in the Tudor and Stuart period was in the process of rapid social change. It was also a society helpless in the face of disease, especially the plague, and fire which thrived upon the primitive living conditions of the people. Its beliefs were directed to 'explain misfortune and to investigate its vigour'.

The medieval church, therefore, had to provide practical as well as other-worldly solutions. But, as Thomas points out:

> It would, of course, be a gross travesty to suggest that the medieval church held out to the laity an organised system of magic designed to bring supernatural remedies to bear upon earthly problems. The Church was other-worldly in its main preoccupation. Most of the magical claims made for religion were parasitic to its teachings, and were more or less vigorously refuted by ecclesiastical leaders (1971 : 46).

The impression put forward by the leaders of the church was of a religious society where any magic that did occur was the result of visitations by the devil. Certainly the extent to which magic played any part in society at this time was never recognised officially. However as Thomas states:

The line between magic and religion is one which it is impossible to draw in many primitive societies; it is equally difficult to recognise in medieval England (1971:50).

He goes further to note that the hold of orthodox religion on the people of England had never been complete, and that certain sections of the population probably had never been religious at all. Referring specifically to notions of secularisation, he says:

Indeed the whole problem may be wrongly posed. We do not know enough about the religious beliefs and practices of our remote ancestors to be certain of the extent to which religious faith and practice have actually declined (1971:173).

After all, in the seventeenth century the sales of almanacs exceeded those of the Bible (1971:294) while witches were still occasionally lynched until well into the nineteenth century (1971:453).

The significance of these observations rests on the assumption that the distinction between magic and religion, as well as that between magic and science (especially medicine), was not made by the 'common people'. Much of Thomas's work is an attempt to show the truth of this assumption. It implies that a concept of religiosity – certainly when used outside the small group within the hierarchy of the church – would need to include magical as well as religious elements.

English witchcraft . . . was neither a religion nor an organisation. Of course there were many pagan survivals – magic walls, calendar customs, fertility rites – just as there were many types of magical activity. But these practices did not usually involve any formal breach with Christianity, and were, as often as not, followed by men and women who would have indignantly repudiated aspersions upon their religious faith (1971:516).

Merton's 'functionally optimum degree of visibility' theory would suggest that the last remark is an accurate reflection of the 'idealisation' constructed by the members of medieval English society. Certainly it was officially religious and the prevalence of magical action and belief went largely unacknowledged by those in authority. MacFarlane notes that witchcraft accusations were not widespread before 1560, and that in Essex (the area he studies in greatest detail) the peak period for suspected witches ran from 1570 to 1600. He concludes:

In Essex, as elsewhere in England, there were informal attacks on suspected witches after prosecutions had ceased at the courts. Old women were thrown into ponds by angry mobs, and people burnt their animals to prevent them being bewitched. But the formal prosecutions ended over fifty years before the Witchcraft Act was repealed in 1736 (1970:200).

One of the more important factors underlying the spate of witchcraft accusations was the considerable social and economic change during the period, rather than any specific recognition of an alternative to the established church. Those in authority accepted the picture of society which they, in a sense, contributed to creating. Magic, witchcraft and astrology were condemned by a church which refused to see how its own rituals and teachings were often used to further these magical ends. As Thomas concludes:

> Even those who stuck to religion sometimes chose to use it for magical purposes upon which the theologians frowned. Yet the Church had all the resources of organised political power on its side, whereas most magical practices were harshly proscribed. The fact that they could still compete so effectively with the recipes of the established church is testimony to their spontaneous basis in the needs of the people (1971:639).

However, the reason for accepting the view of a society constructed by its members, and handed down through its historical records, is not necessarily ignorance of the true state of affairs. Sociologists should be as aware as historians of the methodological pitfalls involved. Many chose to ignore them, especially when discussing the secularisation process. It is assumed, almost blindly, that if contemporary society is to be regarded as secular in some way, then there must have been a time when it can be regarded as having been religious. This is a fundamental methodological error.

Merton suggests, as noted earlier, that an investigator's assessment of the structure and norms of society rests largely with his own values. He can accept or condemn, and is more likely to rely on his own values when studying groups of which he is not a member. Sociologists with neat theories explaining the presence of the secular in contemporary culture may be tempted to accept the authority of, say, the medieval church concerning the state of religiosity in that period. Certainly it would provide a convenient starting point for an analysis of the growth and impact of social, industrial and technological change upon religious institutions. Succumbing to such a temptation can only result in constructing a social myth of the secularisation process.

It should also be noted that in-group membership does not preclude the investigator from accepting an idealised view of its norms and structure. Here there can be no reason for ignorance, and only those who clarify their value position can be excused from sacrificing scientific objectivity. The 'religious' nature of American society, certainly in the institutional sense, is conventionally accepted. However, some sociologists have become aware of the existence of what David Martin (1967:74) calls 'subterranean theologies'. Thus Marcello Truzzi (1972:29) describes the current occult revival[4] as reflecting, in its mass version, a 'pop religion'. Towler (1974) refers to the 'common religion' of the people.

To what extent are these examples of an alternative to existing religious movements? Can they be regarded as evidence of secularisation? Such questions need to be pursued in order to understand the real meaning of religion in contemporary society. Martin (1967:76) is optimistic about the continuing capacity for belief if not for involvement in institutional religion, while Truzzi describes involvement in the occult as 'a leisure-time activity and a fad of popular culture rather than a serious religious involvement in the search for new sacred elements' (1972:29).

Much research in contemporary sociology appears to accept conventionally defined avenues of religiosity as well as the conventionally accepted forms of 'being religious', and thereby indicates the possibility that views of contemporary religiosity have also been idealised.

Merton, in his discussion of 'visibility', suggested that what is *known* about a group may not coincide with what really *occurs* within it. It was suggested at the beginning of this discussion that a dimensional approach to the notion of religiosity may help overcome this difficulty, by concentrating more upon *specific aspects* of structure, norms and behaviour. Such approaches are available in sociological literature, and perhaps the best-known are those of Lenski (1961) and Glock (Glock and Stark 1965, chapter 2). Lenski, using a definition of religion which is inclusive, proposes four major dimensions: associationism; communalism; orthodoxy; and devotionalism. Glock, whose definition of religion is purposely exclusive, suggests five dimensions: experiential; ritualistic; ideological; intellectual; and consequential. In both cases it is possible to construct a profile of religiosity which locates an individual at some point on each dimension. It is acknowledged by both writers that, in Glock's words, there is no reason to assume 'religiosity expressed on one dimension automatically assures it's being manifested on other dimensions as well' (1965:38).

The latest extension of this approach may be found in the works of Morton King (1967), who proposes nine dimensions: creedal assent and personal commitment; participation in congregational activities; personal religious experience; personal ties in the con-

73

gregation; commitment to intellectual search despite doubt; openness to religious growth; dogmatism or extrinsic orientation; financial behaviour and attitude; and talking and reading about religion. These were obtained from factor analysis of data based on three preliminary surveys and 'a careful search of the relevant literature'.

Mervin Verbit (1970) has suggested that these elements often limit the necessary dimensionality; they are not amenable to a single measurement. He suggests that they should be more accurately named 'components', each of which is a variable on one or more 'dimensions'. Each of his six components – ritual, doctrine, emotion, knowledge, ethics and community – has four dimensions: content, frequency, intensity and centrality; and religiosity is thus measured on a 6×4 table.

Verbit does not suggest that religiosity has been analytically exhausted by his reformulation. He, too, sees a problem in postulating a base-line from which to make his measurements. He also sees the difficulties involved in comparing religiosity between different cultures, especially with regard to the relative importance of ritual. He suggests that two crucial errors are often the result of such cross-cultural analysis:

> First, a large number of highly significant items get omitted.
> Second, it is assumed incorrectly that the items that exist in
> both religious traditions have similar meanings and identical
> weights despite differences in their respective contexts (1970: 34).

Thus the problem of idealisation becomes apparent in the discussion of religious dimensions interculturally as well, since the comparison can be between similar societies over large periods of time.

Another difficulty isolated by Verbit centres on the matter of motivation. He notes that O'Dea (1961) has isolated the 'dilemma of mixed motivation' in the sphere of religious institutionalisation, and suggests that Allport's distinction between intrinsic and extrinsic motivation for religiosity be followed. However, here Verbit's discussion tends toward the psychological rather than the sociological, as it does when he notes that behaviour may not reflect sincerity.

The error of idealisation also infiltrates the dimensional analysis of religiosity, through the assumption that the religiosity of a society may be aggregated by the indicators of religiosity among its members.[5] However, as Robertson points out, this approach commits the individualist fallacy and overlooks a whole range of intervening factors, not the least of which revolves around the distinction between a mere summation of overall religiosity as opposed to indication of its intensity (Robertson, 1970:56).

Without some notion of the interrelations between the individual and the wider social structure, this approach to religiosity would appear severely limited. In fact, the major motivating factor behind attempts to construct this taxonomy of religious experience appears to be an attempt to describe individual rather than societal religiosity. Robertson concludes:

> In other words, recent attempts to establish dimensions of religiosity flow not so much from a desire to break down analytically a clearly established or proposed concept of religiosity; but rather to 'add together' available and promising indicators, so arriving *atomistically* at a total, aggregated conception of religiosity (1970:52).

This was made very clear by King, whose source of initial concepts was noted earlier, and whose method clearly indicates the way in which prior orientation can intervene in supposedly objective analysis.[6] Verbit states that isolation and identification of aspects of religiosity happen through sorting an 'array of religious expressions' into sets and, occasionally, through factor analysis of 'some *a priori* characteristic common to the items in each set'. Robertson suggests that most dimensions have been established on a 'fairly *ad hoc* intuitive basis'.

In other words, the dimensional approach to religiosity is open to idealisation, and hence the construction of a social myth, because it is based on conventional definitions located within contemporary, Western industrial society. It assumes that what is 'visible' (in Mertonian terms) can be identified with what *is*. Such an approach, as Robertson makes clear, is only possible through the lack of master-conception, or sociological theory, of religiosity.

Anthropologists have provided 'base-line' material for sociologists of secularisation through their analyses of so-called primitive societies. In the Durkheimian tradition, tribal society is seen as a community and hence a religious group. Durkheim (1915) himself argued that the sacred could only be manifest through the celebration of the group.

A recent analysis by Mary Douglas (1966, 1970) has challenged what has become accepted truth concerning the religiosity of tribal societies. She distinguishes between the individual's experience of society as a bounded social unit, or group, and the order which forms the matrix governing social relations within the group, or the grid. She concludes: 'the secular world view is no modern development, but appears when group boundaries are weak and ego-focused grid is strong' (1970:139). Thus to contrast sacred and secular with ancient and modern is nonsense, and, certainly, secularisation is not solely the product of city life. This fact needs to be grasped by anthropologists who, when coming across an ir-religious tribe, only inquire more deeply in their search for religiosity:

> The idea that primitive man is by nature deeply religious is nonsense. The truth is that all varieties of scepticism, materialism and spiritual fervour are to be found in the range of tribal societies. . . . The illusion that all primitives are pious, credulous and subject to the teaching of priests or magicians has probably done even more to impede our understanding of our own civilisation than it has confused the interpretations of archaeologists dealing with the dead past (1970:x).

Douglas's analysis is concerned to show that the perception and interpretation of symbols in general are socially determined. She, of course, is concerned with religion. However, the point she makes provides a cogent summary of the idealisation process discussed above. Anthropologists will expect to match religion to forms of symbolic behaviour as a result of their own preconceptions or they may even fail to see that religious symbols are absent from the society they study.

It would appear, therefore, that there is some doubt about the accuracy of anthropological representations of 'primitive' religiosity. The theoretical framework for a sociology of secularisation must assume that some societies begin by being secular rather than religious, as well as allowing for the processes of change which, within a short space of time, may transform a society from the secular to the religious state, or vice versa.

In conclusion, the error of idealisation is seen to be manifest in most discussions of secularisation simply through the assumption of a 'base-line' society which is 'really religious'. This methodological error can often result in a process of mythification, if the above-mentioned limitations are not recognised. Certainly, specific analyses of some social situations can provide *micro-sociologies* of the secularisation process. The problem of transformation into a social mythology only arises when these analyses are elevated to the macro-level, with no further analysis of the new difficulties involved. Then specific questions are being answered no longer; the methods used are extended beyond their capabilities; and the ideological element, based on preconceptions and value positions, can easily intrude.

Permeation

The assumption of religious homogeneity within society suggests the second basis for describing the secularisation process as being mythical in character. From the methodological standpoint, it disregards a range of primary, limiting variables, and an attendant host of minute intervening ones. For example, little, if anything, is said about the relative *availability* of religious knowledge or experience within the population. In addition, given that such knowledge or experience is available to, at least, a section of the population, such factors as selective *perception,* the variety of *interpretation* and differential *salience,* tend to be overlooked.[7]

The purpose of the discussion which follows is to indicate the degree to which availability, perception, interpretation and salience may be affected by intervening variables. Such a discussion will be necessarily selective, and an attempt will be made to choose variables in which important work which cannot be described as peripheral has already been done. It is hoped that this will underline the mythological nature of the analysis of secularisation. The following variables will be discussed: socialisation; deprivation; style; geographical location; political factors; and available alternatives.

Socialisation

The concept of religious socialisation involves the *a priori* notion that religion, religiosity, or religious behaviour, is learnt rather than inherited or somehow present at birth. It is also broad enough to encompass the formal aspects of the process, such as religious education in schools and Sunday Schools, and the more indirect influences, such as those of the immediate family, the peer group and the mass media.

One method of looking at the problems involved is to approach them developmentally. Thus, the less formal factors are more likely to be important during the early years of a child's life. Parental control would appear to be a major one affecting religious socialisation, especially when linked with affective support.

A recent American study by Weigert and Thomas (1970), for example, found that where persons had been socialised under conditions of strong parental control and strong affective support, they were more likely to accept their parent's beliefs and behaviour patterns, including those in the religious sphere. In conditions of weak parental control and strong affective support, the likelihood of religious conformity also tended to be high. These results applied particularly to the early pre-school years of a child's life.

In the early years of schooling, the child's conceptual apparatus probably has developed sufficiently to allow it to absorb more formal instruction (Piaget and Inhelder, 1958). However there is some doubt about exactly *what* is being absorbed under such conditions. Thus Goldman (1964) suggests that a young child's ability to grasp the sort of material taught in Sunday School is often quite distinct from its religious content. He quotes young children as interpreting 'holy ground' (in a reference to Moses and the Burning Bush) as 'ground with holes in it', 'hot ground' as 'ground on which grass is growing'. He suggests that it requires the child to have the mental age of a teenager before the abstract religious ideas can become meaningful.

Peer group influences become more important in the period up to adolescence, and the influence of formal organisations such as schools and churches plays an increasingly significant role. However this influence will tend to support many of the patterns formed in earlier stages.

This is certainly true if the major variable of social class is used to order the evidence. It is not necessary to go further than the work of Bernstein on linguistic codes to see how important early socialisation becomes in assessing the religious knowledge and understanding of the adolescent. Bernstein (1965) suggests that only middle-class children have access to the 'elaborated' speech code which allows them to handle conceptual notions such as uniqueness, or individuality, and which gives them the ability to deal with abstract concepts. In this way, the social class of the individual may act to limit his religiosity in a variety of variables, including the *availability* of religious phenomena, and their *perception* and *interpretation*.

The 'restricted' speech code is much more related to ritual, and often unexplained action (see Douglas, 1970: chapter 2). Thus, answers to the question: Why must I do such-and-such? are likely to be couched in concrete, positional terms, such as: Because I said so, or, Because you're a boy. Ritual, rather than abstract ideas, becomes characteristic of certain kinds of socialisation processes, and is often exemplified among working-class groups. A secularisation process, concerned with abstractions, which omits mention of this differential socialisation, but which attempts a societal generalisation, can be accused of propagating the kind of social myth already discussed. Similarly, undue emphasis on the ritual element in religious change can produce the same results.

Finally, it is worth noting that the view of the secularisation process as 'segmentation' uses the fact of imperfect or partial socialisation as the mainspring for change in the religious sphere, and hence as a possible initiator of secularisation. Doubts were expressed about the adequacy of this theoretical model, especially in terms of the operational measures of the degree of imperfection required to 'trigger' change. However, at least the possibility of inadequate or imperfect socialisation into a particular world view is recognised in this theory of the secularisation process, and to overlook it as a possible factor in explaining the differential permeations of religion in society would be unwise. Thus a major variable may be just sheer ignorance of the various tenets and dogma associated with the religious culture in question.

This discussion has been set within the framework of Western culture and religion. In Japan, similar principles will apply, although their concrete manifestations may well differ. Thus, the process of socialisation into ritual is probably greater among Japanese families of all categories. This relates to their concept of morality being equivalent in many ways to etiquette. Thus Norbeck (1970:116) quotes Leslie A. White as saying that the border between them is unclear. Etiquette relates to class in Japanese society, but the concept of class differs slightly from its Western counterpart. 'Men, women, adults, children, married, widowed, divorced etc. are their classes.'

A code of etiquette defines each class in terms of a pattern of behaviour, and imposes sanctions in order to maintain its integrity. Often such penalties are couched in terms of supernatural sanctions, the imposition of which results in guilt and fear. Thus, the situation in Japan, at least during its pre-industrial era, was much more complex than that found in Western industrial society. However Norbeck does note that recent economic and technical changes within Japan have resulted in a greater 'westernisation' of the class system, leaving the way open for failings within the socialisation process similar to those already described.

Deprivation

Another important variable which needs to be taken into acount before generalisations about religious homogeneity in a population can be made is relative deprivation. David Aberle states:

> Relative deprivation is defined as the negative discrepancy between legitimate expectation and actuality. Where an individual or a group has a particular expectation and furthermore where this expectation is considered to be a proper state of affairs, and where something less than that expectation is fulfilled, we may speak of relative deprivation (Aberle: 1962).

79

Aberle goes on to note that standards of comparison are with the past, the future, and with other groups. He suggests an elaborate 24-cell table covering the relationship between these standards and four groups of deprivation (possessions, status, behaviour and worth), each of which can be either personal or related to the group. However he limits his analysis artificially by suggesting that personal deprivation can be eliminated because of its 'trivial' significance for social movements as a result of necessity of finding others with similar problems.

Glock and Stark (1965), in their analysis of deprivation theory on the origin and evolution of religious groups, disagree with Aberle about the significance of individual forms of deprivation. They criticise the position of economic deprivation as the major variable. They suggest that, in addition to economic deprivation, at least four other types can be discerned. Each of these will have different implications for the type of religious movement which results.

Social deprivation arises out of the differential distribution of highly regarded attributes such as prestige, power, status, etc. Organismic deprivation relates to physical or mental disadvantages and other such stigmatising or disabling traits. Ethical deprivation refers to 'value conflicts between the ideals of society and those of individuals or groups', either through discrepancies or the detection of negative latent functions. Finally, psychic deprivation occurs when individuals find themselves in a state of acute anomie.

Glock and Stark go on to suggest the form of religious groups which tend to arise from each kind of deprivation, and this is summarised in Table 3.1.

TABLE 3.1

Type of deprivation	Form of religious group
1 Economic	Sect
2 Social	Church
3 Organismic	Healing movement
4 Ethical	Reform movement
5 Psychic	Cult

Source: Taken from Glock and Stark (1965:259).

The significance of their analysis lies in the pin-pointing of conditions for the rise of religious movements which may be independent of any secularisation process. Extreme socio-economic or personal conditions can arise outside more general trends. However, if these trends are described as part of a process of secularisation, and the exceptional conditions actually do give rise to religious movements *because* of these trends, then the mythological element in the process becomes apparent.

It is not necessary to go further than the three main examples of secularisation, which were explored in greater detail in the first section, to see how this situation can arise. Thus in secularisation seen as decline, a lack of religiosity, in terms of either religious rituals or organisations, could involve the development of *perceived* deprivations in the ethical and psychic spheres. On the one hand those groups which enjoyed high status by belonging to established religious groups, could well suffer from social deprivation as defined by Glock and Stark, when these religious groups experienced a state of decay.

Similar possibilities arise with secularisation seen as a process of generalisation, and with what is conventionally seen as secularisation itself. Organismic deprivation is at least likely to result from secularisation processes, but economic deprivation can be a by-product in all instances, either directly through the threat to livelihoods, or indirectly by changes in the legitimating structures of morality. Thus generalisation may result in greater opportunities for exploitation solely because the normative controls cease to be closely supervised. The development of 'secular' society through the move from community will have the effect of removing a 'safety net' from many individuals whose problems would normally have been absorbed by relations and friends.

In this way, an unintended but significant by-product of some major theories of the secularisation process may well be the development of new religious movements whose strength arises from perceived deprivation, itself a product of the secularisation process. However, it should always be remembered that deprivation 'theory' is open to tautology (Wallis, 1975).

Relative deprivation theory can be applied cross-culturally and used outside Western society. Fujio Ikado (1968) describes the 'new religions' of Japan as featuring 'horizontal' rather than 'vertical' social development as a constraint to the old, established religions. Thus the *Soka Gakkai* movement started among the economically under-privileged, immigrant, unskilled workers in Tokyo, and then spread to the low-ranking white-collar workers who became dissatisfied with the system, and were, presumably, exhibiting ethical deprivation. Much of the development of the 'new religious' stemmed from a breakdown of community ties due to the rapid process of post-war industrialisation in Japan,[8] or, in

81

other words, from the process of secularisation as described in Category III above.

In conclusion, it would seem that the rise of new religious movements can be a by-product of the processes of secularisation as they have been described, and, hence, can limit their applicability unless such possibilities are included within the theoretical framework. Certainly, to suggest, even by implication, that religious movements cannot develop during, or as a result of, the secularisation process, is to propagate the process as a social myth.

Style

The concept of relative deprivation is not far removed from that of strain as suggested by Erich Goode (1968). He accepts that religion is related in some way to the uncertainty, grief and tragedy of social life, and follows Parsons in describing these as 'points of maximum strain and tension'. Such strain is present in the lives of all individuals in society, but more so, Goode argues, in some lives than others. It seems unquestionably more likely to be present at the bottom rather than at the top of the class structure:

> Religion, then, can be seen as a response to this greater strain. A higher level of religiosity can be expected of lower status individuals because religion attempts to alleviate the strain, frustrations, anxieties and uncertainties that exist, in greater quantity and intensity, among the lower classes. Being religious is an attempt to mitigate the greater difficulties inherent in lower class life (Goode, 1968: 6).

Goode goes on to suggest a paradox: although those of low status should be more religious, they appear, in the sense of organisational participation, to be less so than those of middle status. However the *intensity* of their commitment is much higher.

The solution to this paradox lies in the introduction of another variable – participation in all kinds of organisation, be it church or non-church. Middle status individuals are more likely to be members of more non-church organisations than those of lower status levels. David Martin makes much the same point when he remarks that:

> Modern churches are clearly middle and lower-middle-class associations producing one tangential relationship among others – and that not perhaps the most important. They are the religious variety of club for the clubable classes (Martin, 1967: 106).

This, suggests Goode, seems to indicate that the various status groups within society are best described as having a distinctive religious *style*. He says:

> If we were to typify the working class person according to his
> religious style, then, we would say that he is a good deal more
> likely to be internally involved in his church and concerned
> with the importance of religion in his life. On the other hand,
> he attends religious services less. Likewise, he is less active
> in formal organisations. . . . The middle-class person, on the
> other hand, is less concerned with religion, less psychologically
> identified with the church, but is more active in its formal
> programs. He has, we could say, a different 'style' of religious
> sociation (Goode, 1968:11).

Hence, for a large part of the population, religion can be said to lose its sacred quality because participation in organisations becomes a key variable. It would, however, be a mistake to imagine that this occurs throughout society, or that it forms an example of the process of secularisation.

Many of the 'new religions' of Japan also provide 'clubs for the clubable classes'. There are distinct differences between the instrumentally oriented movements, such as *Soka Gakkai*, whose appeal is to the deprived and disenchanted, and the more urbane, expressive movements such as *Rissho Koseikai* which appeal more to the traditional middle class. The central organising rationale for the former appears to be some attempt to change the system, perhaps through political action. The latter appear to concentrate more on elaborate centres for worship and entertainment, and often compete with each other in terms of the number of ping-pong tables rather than doctrinal interpretation. Charles Allen has made the following observations: [9]

> There is outside Osaka, a strange new city, superbly
> landscaped, with large, often ultra-modern buildings set among
> lakes and hills and – rather strangely – a 72 holed golf course.
> I'm told they even have 600 girl caddies to go with it.
> Dominating the skyline is an enormous cement sculpture, the
> PL Peace Tower, rising to a point nearly six hundred feet
> above the ground. This City of Art, as it has been called,
> complete with sculptures and Picassos, piped music, coloured
> fountains and poetry gardens, is the headquarters of P. L.
> Kyodan, the Church of Perfect Liberty. . . . At first, P. L. faced
> considerable derision, often being described in the press as

the 'golfing religion' or the 'businessman's religion', but it is now gaining support from the middle classes.

While this discussion has accepted the distinction between social status categories little has been said about individuals who may be socially mobile. Demerath (1965) notes that a person's status can be ambiguous, especially when he suffers from 'status discrepancy'. He goes on:

> Just as a traditional church may offer a more rewarding orientation for those of low status, it may offer a more consistent orientation for those with high status discrepancy (1965:xxiii).

This additional factor provides yet another kind of religious style, with an emphasis on the content and stability of the religious world view being offered as well as the desire to be a member of a movement which is unambiguously of the 'correct' status.

Hence, religious 'style' appears to play an important part in any analysis of religious change. Such factors as the stratification system, and the kind and extent of social mobility within society, need to be known prior to any generalisation being made about secularisation theories. Without this information, creation of social myth becomes a real possibility in their formation.

Geographical factors

The notion that a geographical locality could have its own 'religious personality' was first explored by French religious sociologists. Thus Boulard's analysis of the geographical pattern of French religious practice, especially in the Garonne valley diocese, showed that little had changed over the previous century.[10] He concluded that religious stability was greater than usually thought, that the concept of dechristianisation was not new, and that each geographical locality can be said to have an enduring religious personality of its own (Boulard, 1960: chapter 6).

This relationship has been found to hold elsewhere in Europe. Vogt (1966), discussing Norwegian Protestantism, notes that available evidence suggests the importance of geographical factors in understanding differences in 'religiosity', particularly in relation to communication facilities, population density, prevailing types of economic life, etc. Gustaffson (1965), with even more limited data, also feels that such patterns could emerge in a study of Scandinavian Protestantism. Some observers have even suggested that there are two European stronghold areas (Protestant and Catholic), divided geographically by a complex of hill masses and river valleys which are conducive to the development of small politico-religious units of an absolutist variety.[11]

In a recent English study, John Gay (1971), using community studies and census data, found that allegiance to the Anglican church is greatest in 'those geographically isolated areas where village life will have experienced least modification'. He found in addition that there was a belt of strong Catholic practice running from Lancashire to Warwickshire which was broken only as recently as 1962, and that the most significant growth has been within sixty miles of London. The greater part of the Catholic population of England seems to be found in urban rather than rural areas.

The Free Church of Scotland, with its narrow, Calvinist outlook, seems to predominate in the Highlands of north and north-west Scotland according to John Highet (1960), while the Church of Scotland broadly covers the whole country. This religious personality of the Highlands still appears to be significantly rooted in geographical factors.

Little work has been done in North America by way of ecclesiastical cartography. However, Gaustad,[12] who relies to a great extent on the *Yearbook of American Churches,* has noted that:

> In 1650 American Religion displayed a high degree of geographical unity, with Congregationalists in New England, Baptists in Rhode Island, Dutch Reformed in New York, Presbyterians on Long Island, Lutherans in Delaware, Roman Catholics in Maryland, and Anglicans in Virginia . . . (and) even in 1950, clear geographic patterns of ecclesiastical regionalism could be discerned.

A state-by-state plotting of denominations was carried out by Hotchkins in Cincinnati.[13] He found that the churches of the major denominations generally drew members from fairly small, tight-knit geographical parishes, while the smaller denominations drew members from more deprived parishes. In a survey of the relationship between church members and their churches in one community, the concept of a 'natural area', served by a church irrespective of denominational labels, evolved.

Much of the contemporary material on Japanese religion has been concerned with understanding and describing the phenomenon of the 'new religions'. As such, these studies are not particularly concerned with the geographical location or specific religious beliefs. However, the post-war period of industrialisation appears to have transformed Japan from an agrarian, rural society to an industrial, urban one.

The position and strength of the 'new religions' is, in many ways, related to the periods in which they developed initially as well as to their specific appeal in the present. Thus *Rissho Koseikai* developed before the period of industrialisation and still maintains a hold on the rural middle class, appealing only to the relatively well-to-do small business groups in cities.

The *Soka Gakkai*, on the other hand, is a post-industrialisation phenomenon appealing specifically to the lower middle class or young, labouring class. Buddhism and Tenrikyo still maintain a strong foundation in traditional rural areas. The majority of the 'new religions' are, however, predominantly urban in character.

Thus, in conclusion, the rural–urban factor appears to exert a profound influence of religiosity in most industrial societies. This rural–urban difference does not necessarily exhaust the range of variation uncovered by sociographic analysis, and some evidence has been discovered to suggest the possible presence of 'natural areas' of religiosity or areas with 'religious personalities' which relate to geographical rather than local factors. Certainly such possibilities are relatively well established, and should be incorporated into theories of the secularisation process.

In the main, apart from those processes which involve a rural–urban continuum, most theories of secularisation tend to assume that, like Japan, Western society can be accurately described as an urban-industrial complex. However, even Ikado uses the words 'in a sense' when talking of Japan, and to suggest that such differences do *not* occur is to indulge in the myth-making process.

Political factors

Analysis under this broad heading is concerned with the extent to which political intervention in religious affairs can affect the homogeneous nature of religiosity in society. It is assumed generally, as noted in the earlier section concerning religious 'style', that there are class differences in religiosity. It is also assumed that low status individuals are most likely to find religious sects appealing than high status individuals whose interests are in the more established churches and denominations.

These are, what can best be described as micro-political factors. Thus, in the UK, some large percentage of members of the working class vote Conservative, a phenomenon of great interest to sociologists (Mackenzie and Silver, 1968). However, most studies seem to indicate that the British working class is also religiously apathetic

(Martin, 1967: chapters 2–4). This sort of paradox may be resolved only through a thorough investigation of the impact of politics on the life-style of the individual in British society. Certainly, the question of alternatives to membership of religious movements, which will be followed up below, would seem relevant.

On the macro-level, the difficulties become easier to identify. A significant factor would appear to be the separation of church and state. Certainly, the taking over of Shinto by the Japanese monarchy before the Second World War did much to influence certain kinds of religious behaviour. This became even more true with the identification between State Shinto and Nationalism (Bellah, 1958). A by-product of this move was, of course, the banning of many other religious movements, which continued to flourish underground and rose into full flower after the war. Now, with the division between church and state grounded in Japan's constitution, a different kind of religiosity appears to have flourished. However, the problem for students of secularisation lies in comparability, and the extent to which they can say that pre-war Japan was more, or less, 'religious' (in some particular sense) than contemporary Japan. Has the division between church and state *really* resulted in a process of secularisation?

Much the same problem, though reversed, faces the sociologist who discusses countries behind the Iron Curtain, where religion, at least in any organised sense, is largely proscribed. To what extent can these societies be regarded as having undergone religious secularisation?

In some cases, separation of church and state appears to have resulted in an *increase* in religiosity. This is the case in the USA as evidenced by the religious pluralism which there prevails. This is a natural by-product of the freedom of worship which is written into the constitution, as well as a reflection of the cultural heterogeneity of American society. However, it is difficult to describe America as a secular society, if the indices of religiosity include number and variety of religious movements and organisations, regular attendance, membership and belief in stated doctrines (Parsons, 1964).

The kinds of freedom which Americans regard as their constitutional heritage – life, liberty and the pursuit of happiness – can also contradict those of freedom of religious belief. Thus Jehovah's Witnesses have been persecuted to some extent, because of their beliefs, including their disinclination to go to war (Stroup, 1945). In fact David Moberg goes so far as to state that:

Religious discrimination ... has been apparent in the treatment of Quakers, Jews, Unitarians, Catholics, Baptists, Mormons, Jehovah's Witnesses, Hutterites, Amish, and other groups at various times and places (1962:455).

Certainly government intervention is not precluded, if the interests of the majority are to be safeguarded. Thus, in the state of Victoria in Australia, the Scientology movement has been officially banned from operating on the grounds that it is propagating psychologically harmful material.

In conclusion, it would seem that the political variable may be of sufficient importance to affect the normal processes of religious development. A variety of political factors may intervene, at either the micro- or the macro-level. These factors may not be in themselves part of a process of secularisation, but they may help or hinder it. To assume their absence is, however, to be in danger of propagating a social myth.

Available alternatives

The importance of alternatives to religion in any discussion of the process of secularisation cannot be ignored, especially if the reasons for joining such alternatives can be identified as unrelated to religion. The possibility that political organisations form an example of such alternatives was suggested above. However, other alternatives are available, and the list would include social clubs, adult education and sport on the organisational level; or alcoholism, suicide and insanity on the more individual one.

Glock and Stark (1965; chapter 10) found, in studying religiosity and social class in Britain, that 'radical solutions for economic deprivation imply a lessening of religious involvement'. They also found, in comparing Britain with the USA and some European countries, that the greater the left-right dispersion of parties within a political system, the greater the differences in church attendance between the party furthest left and the party furthest right.[14]

These studies led them to conclude that political rather than religious solutions to various problems will occur only under particular circumstances:

> In the case of economic, social and organismic deprivation . . . religious resolutions are more likely to occur where the nature of the deprivation is inaccurately perceived or those experiencing the deprivation are not in a position to work directly at eliminating the causes. The resolution is likely to be secular under the opposite conditions – where the nature of the deprivation is correctly assessed by those experiencing it and

they have, or feel they have, the power, or feel they can gain the power, to deal with it directly (1965:249).

In the case of ethical and psychic deprivation, either solution may be sought, depending, to a large extent, on the exact nature of the problem, and the culture in which it has become manifest.

The significance of available alternatives to religion in contemporary society has also been explored by Berger (1969a) in his analogy with the 'market model' of a plurality of world views. He suggests that the process of secularisation has resulted in all religious movements becoming organisationally similar, and in their competing with one another. Luckmann (1967) actually takes this view to its logical conclusion in suggesting that all movements, religious or secular, are in this position. Hence, the importance of organisational factors in influencing the decision to join arises.

This is well illustrated in Japan and its 'new religions' which, as noted earlier, often compete with one another on the level of social clubs rather than religious organisations. Similarly some, like *Soka Gakkai* compete (successfully) with political parties, and presumably, with paternalistic industrial organisations. Hence the significance of alternatives to religion being available in society is not to be overlooked in the desire to establish a theoretical rather than mythical account of the secularisation process.

The preceding discussions have shown that such major factors as salience, interpretation, perception and availability all need to be included, and allowed for, in any theory of secularisation, if it is not to become mythical in character. Certainly they dispel any suggestion of religious homogeneity within society, and underline the simplistic nature of generalisations based upon such an assumption. In all cases, Toulmin's criterion for identifying the start of the myth-making process appears satisfied. Generalisations involving religious homogeneity necessitate either ignoring the existence of the variables discussed, or taking one or more of them and distorting or extending the usage to a society-wide perspective. The various processes of secularisation discussed in the earlier chapters all seem to accept religious homogeneity at one level or another. It is suggested that by doing so they provide solid evidence for propagating a social myth of secularisation.

Categorisation

This section will be mainly concerned to show that conventional definitions, in the form of religious categories, have substantially contributed to raising the process of secularisation to the status of

89

G

social myth. The underlying ideological commitment of users of, for example, church-sect typologies, will be clarified in the light of their discussions of the secularisation process.

In the *decline* thesis, much of the discussion centres around the changes which have occurred from earlier historic periods (often in terms of sacred to secular, or other-worldly to this-worldly, orientations), in which the main religious organisation in society was identifiable as the church. This discussion is often explicitly based upon the analyses of Troeltsch (1931) and Weber (1963), who isolated certain specific characteristics of 'churchness' in order to analyse change in the institutional framework. Such characteristics are for example: membership by birth, acceptance of the state and existing order, the necessity of sacraments, presence of religious office holders, etc. However, as will be suggested below in the specific discussion of church-sect typologies, the concept of church was envisaged primarily as an ideal-type and not as an extreme type. Hence the postulated continuum of high and low institutional participation tends to form the basis of the decline theories.

Wilson (1966) suggests that his starting point for the secularisation process is a concept of the church 'which acquired its full meaning and realisation in European Feudal society'. His analysis is based explicitly upon Weber and Troeltsch, and he contrasts it with the sect. Wilson has his own theory of sect development which, though based on routinisation, does not necessarily mean secularisation. For example, he notes the changes which have occurred in charismatic presentations *after* society has become secularised. He also suggests that schism is a major source of sect development. Finally, he notes that the sect need not necessarily move out of the sectarian stage in the second generation, and suggests that it is most likely not to do so if of the conversionist type, and that when it does, the outcome may not be the formation of a denomination. It is a more general process of secularisation which reduces churches to sects and denominations, not some inner dynamic on their part.

> When large numbers effectively ceased to be religious all
> religious movements were reduced to the status of denominations
> and sects (Wilson, 1966:222).

This process is more difficult where a concept of the medieval church remains, so that secularisation in America 'drained the religious content, without radically affecting the form, of religious institutions'. Wilson is arguing, therefore, that ecumenism and liturgicalism are the strategies that eroded church-like organisations sink to in order to 'restore the security of the past'. It is a response to the danger of the churches becoming sects. But, throughout his analysis, he admits to using a conventional definition of church, as suggested by Troeltsch, which is rooted in the Christian ethic, and which even Wilson suggests, when talking about the persistence of the concept of church, might be described as fictional. His main indices of contrast are size, area of control and level of commitment. Secularisation is seen as a decline in all three levels. Categorisation involves Wilson in the suggestion that the church, which is high on the first two levels, but low on the last, is in some way 'more religious' than the sect which establishes the opposite characteristics.

This would appear to be in direct contrast with the church-sect typologists who argue that commitment to the religious ideals should be the major ordering variable, and that the sect is 'really religious' while the church and denomination represent secularised values.

Sorokin (1966: 17) also identifies 'The decline of the Christian church as a social institution' as evidence of the secularisation process. This 'fragmentation' of the church of the Middle Ages has resulted in a 'multitude of different denominations, sects and cults'. Like Wilson, Sorokin utilises the Troeltschian church-sect analysis to suggest that schism, resulting from routinisation, is the source of sectarian origins, and that the inability of sects to grow into churches stems from the 'advanced secularisation of the whole socio-cultural life of the west'.

The paradox of assigning a high value, in terms of religiosity, to church-like rather than sect-like organisations, can be traced, once again, to categorisation. The church of the Middle Ages provides the basis of the Troeltschian ideal-type. But, this ideal-type, when taken as an extreme type, involves a contrast with the concept of 'non-church'. For the decline theorists 'non-church' appears to involve the growth of sectarian confusion, which then becomes identified with the 'non-religious'. By implication, and sometimes even explicitly, the high point of *religiosity* is taken to be temporally and spatially identical with the extreme type of church organisation. Sorokin, as noted earlier, talks of the 'religious animated Medieval Christian culture and society', in contrast with the supposedly non-religious modern culture and society. Rarely does he mean that medieval Christian culture and society, unlike contemporary culture society, was centred on megalithic, institutionalised religious structures. Most users of the church-sect typology would suggest that this represented a necessarily diluted, and hence less extreme, form of religiosity – the opposite end of the continuum.

A similar difficulty presents itself in the *segmentation* theory of secularisation, as propounded by Berger (1969a) with its emphasis on the removal of sectors of society from the dominance of religious institutions and symbols. The overriding plausibility structure which forms the basis of this removal in Christian society is manifested in the church, and its transformation to market pluralism comes from the development of industrial society:

> The original 'carrier' of secularisation is the modern economic process that is, the dynamic of industrial capitalism
> (Berger, 1969a : 109).

The origins, however, are to be found with the Judaeo-Christian tradition and secularisation was only held back through the strength of Catholicism. The 'disenchantment of the world' begins in the Old Testament and is brought to fruition in the 'secularising potency of protestantism'.

This analysis indicates the heavy reliance placed by Berger upon conventional definitions of the church as providing the overall plausibility structure within non-secular society. The form and structure again fit well with Troeltsch's original formulation. The implication is that the overwhelming impact of this plausibility structure, which supposedly entered into all aspects of life, was the same as that of the Christian church at its height (the Middle Ages), which in turn was the same as that of a highly 'religious' society. Modern society, with differentiation resulting from the logic of industrialism, provides a market in plausibility structures, such structures being best described as denominations and sects. Here the outcome of the secularisation process follows closely that of religious decline. But Berger (1969a: 6), as already noted, limits his 'plausibility structures' to conventionally defined religious institutions, and thus reveals his use of categorisation.

The concept of the church-defined plausibility structure takes over from his original analysis of the sacred referent for the plausibility structure, so that its lessening importance in the face of increasing industrialisation overlooks the possibility of there remaining in existence a 'sacred' cosmos at a much higher level of generality (see the discussion of *generic* religion above). Berger therefore commits the double error of abandoning the logic of his earlier analysis and of constructing a social myth, with the resultant transformation of the plausibility structure from the 'sacred' to the 'institutionally sacred' as conventionally defined.

Bellah's (1964) analysis of the differentiation theory of secularisation appears to stumble, in much the same way, over the provision of a theoretical account, on the one hand, and the relating of it to historic reality, on the other. The result is a change in the underlying mode of discourse to the non-theoretical: social differentiation will involve differentiation of the integrating normative structure.

However this does not necessarily involve a differentiation of the institutional manifestations, as Bellah, himself, is aware. In his discussion of primitive and archaic religious forms he sees the move as being *towards* an overall institutionalisation rather than away from it. Thus, it is suggested that Bellah works with two distinctive indices of the evolution of religion. The first is a theoretical account, based on social differentiation, while the second is an historical account, based on received definitions of religion and religiosity.

The high point of institutionalised religion comes in the 'historic religion' phase with its differentiated religious collectivities and well-established hierarchies. His 'evolution' therefore goes through an initial period of differentiation, in which no institutional manifestations are available, or during which a broad and all-embracing institutional structure is being developed. This inconsistency can only be the result of categorisation, because the outcome of the secularisation process is seen, not in relation to the original mythopoeic forms of primitive religion, but in relation to historic religion. Bellah talks not of the absence of *mythical* beliefs, but of an infinite variation of *religious* beliefs within a pluralistic differentiation of structural forms. Hence his evolutionary continuum runs from historic to modern religion, and not, as his original theoretical justification would suggest, from archaic to modern religion.

This is a difficulty that Bellah and Parsons overcome in their discussions of *generic* religion, because here the medieval church is seen as one step in the process of differentiation of religious beliefs to higher levels of generality, and modern religion is manifested in terms which include institutional forms but which transcend them in reference.

Herberg (1967b), in his analysis, moves away from the tri-faith system, and suggests that the operational religion of American society operates on the highly differentiated (that is in normative terms) and generalised level of the 'American way'. Bellah's suggestion that his own concept of civil religion stands alongside this conception fails to convince because of his vagueness about its exact nature. Both Herberg and Bellah seem to be attempting to explain the existence, on the one hand, of institutional religion and, on the other, of a lack of normative religious underpinning to American society. Herberg's thesis, in terms of the secularisation process, is the more successful for being better documented. However, like Bellah, he is offering the 'American way' as the secular end of the secularisation continuum. The process of differentiation in religious terms ends with the analysis of the contemporary scene. Conventional definitions of the religious become categorised as extreme types, and contrast with equally conventional definitions of undifferentiated archaic forms of religiosity to provide a spurious continuum of religious development which may provide a *general description* of religious change, but because they are unable to step outside its received definitions, cannot suggest an *explanatory theory*.

This problem is magnified in that form of the secularisation thesis described as routinisation. This form of secularisation will be discussed in greater detail than the other forms because it emphasises the relevance for them all of the Troeltsch-Weber distinction between church and sect.

The error of categorisation, seen as the identification of religiosity or religion with an extreme type, is best illustrated in the continuing debate concerning the church-sect typologies. Troeltsch's original analysis was in the form of ideal types rather than an attempt to describe empirical reality (1931:340ff). He specifically stated that not only are they independent constructs which do not form a dichotomy, but they are both analytically related types which share common origins in Christianity. It is Niebuhr who suggests that sects are transitory and postulates a continual movement between the two polar types of sect and church. Denominations are then seen as falling somewhere along the continuum, hence opening the door to the whole area of church-sect typologising.

Gustafson (1967), also noting that Niebuhr's (1954) contribution was a significant source of error, goes further and suggests that he was responsible for the reification of the concepts in terms of 'existential' categories. By linking them in a dichotomy, Niebuhr was forced to emphasise those aspects of Troeltsch's definition which suggested that church and sect were polar opposites. In fact, Gustafson notes two distinct polarities in Troeltsch's analysis: the objective-subjective means of grace, and the universalistic-particularistic concept of membership. The resulting possible combinations form the title of his article. What is important, however, is that Troeltsch's work gained strength from the accidental correlation, up to the time of Reformation, between universalism and objectivity, on the one hand, and particularism and subjectivity, on the other. Gustafson suggests that the difficulties of satisfactorily applying the church-sect continuum to the period since the Reformation stem from the ideological reliance upon these correlations 'without regard for its base in Christian doctrine'.

Benton Johnson (1963), noting that an important element of sectness would seem to be the acceptance or rejection of the social order of which it is part, criticises the church-sect typology for this major theoretical and empirical error. Those elements which make it up, he suggests, may have been empirically related, that is, found together at the same time and in the same place, but they need not necessarily be logically related. Hence the typology is not based upon the true dimensions.

A further point has been made by Russell Dynes (1955, 1957) who notes that the typology may need a completely different construction when applied to individuals rather than organisations. These aspects are further investigated by Goode (1967) who isolates three such elements. The first, formal church participation, suggests that church oriented individuals score higher than sect-like individuals with regard to formal church activities. 'Ritual is seen as manifestation and reaffirmation of secularity. . . .' Goode finds the implication, namely that a complete absence of formal participation and ritual shows a high degree of sectness, absurd. This is especially true when the supposed correlation between formal participation and 'being middle class' is borne in mind. He concludes that:

> Specifically religious variables in this relationship, then,
> appeared to be a figment of more direct relationships between
> class and organisational participation (1967:73).

Similar difficulties arise with the relative importance of formal religious observance, which seems to be more class related than church-sect related.

The third example, friendships and communal attachments, is related to the *Gemeinschaft-Gesellschaft* dimension. Here the greatest communal attachments, both in extent and depth, are said to be among the most sect-like parishioners because of the informality of sectarian friendship patterns, and the impersonality of the churches. But, as Goode notes, the

> notion that lower class individuals have closer, warmer and
> more extensive friendships even within churches and even within
> 'sect-like' churches, than do middle class parishioners, is totally
> incorrect (1967:74).

The confusion arises from a conflation of two indices: the degree of concentration and the degree of extensiveness. Goode argues that many writers, especially Demerath, have regarded the two as equivalent when it is quite possible that they relate inversely. He concludes, therefore, that 'most of what passes for definition today is merely a sense of empirically related characteristics'.

Demerath (1967) accepts much of Goode's general criticism of the uses of the church-sect type typology, though he defends the theoretical status of the church-sect dynamic by comparing it to a model of change similar to Marxism and the social sciences. But

95

he does accept the parochial element in its usage that has tended to make the distinction culture-bound. Further he suggests that a more telling criticism lies with it being 'institution-bound and institution-binding' within the general framework of Western society itself. With a few exceptions, 'the sociology of religion has tied itself to a decrepit theoretical wagon and choked in the dust of its tracks'.

It was noted earlier that the routinisation form of the secularisation process is rooted in a common usage definition of primary terms, ample evidence of which is provided in the preceding discussion. It has been suggested that Troeltsch, with his specific concern with Christian ethics (unlike Weber, whose church-sect distinctions were made in general terms of inclusiveness-exclusiveness) and Niebuhr who transformed two ideal-types into the poles of a continuum, both worked with conventional definitions of church and sect based on historical reality. By doing so, they identified numerous elements which, though empirically related, have little or no connection. The result is that their relevance to modern society is very limited. Eister (1967) goes further to accuse Troeltsch of emphasising certain characteristics which constituted 'an open invitation, if not a demand, for subjective, value-laden definitions'.

Hence four main conclusions emerge:
1 Church-sect is culture-bound and based on historical accident;
2 Church-sect dimensions are not unitary;
3 Church-sect is not a continuum;
4 Church-sect is based on conventional definitions of religion and religiosity, and is therefore institution-bound and institution-binding.

These conclusions underline the limitations to the usefulness of church-sect typologising for the study of the secularisation process. The major ordering variable is taken as a move from concern with 'other-worldly' to concern with 'this-worldly' things. It is suggested that all sects necessarily accommodate to the world through the process of routinisation in order to continue to exist. As a result they may change in form to institutionalised sects or denominations as well as to churches. Different writers see the final outcome of the secularisation process as ranging from the church to the tri-faith system.

The process of routinisation involves changes in other indices such as implicitness, particularism and subjectivity. Most writers assume that the cult precedes the sect in the secularisation process by providing the most positive evidence of these indices.[15] Nelson has suggested that this view is mistaken, and he provides grounds for distinguishing them from other religious groups:

(a) Cults are groups based upon mystical, psychic or ecstatic experiences.
(b) They represent a fundamental break with the religious tradition of the society in which they arise.
(c) They are concerned mainly with the problems of individuals rather than social groups (Nelson, 1968: 354).

He then argues that Troeltsch's description of cults, which contributed the initial dynamic to the view of church-sect as a process of secularisation, is not borne out empirically. An absence of any form of permanence is not necessarily the overriding feature of cults, and Nelson further argues that 'groups distinguished by their three major criteria may develop an organisational structure and may survive for longer periods'. Unlike earlier commentators, such as Johnson and Martin, Nelson sees cults as syncretic, and hence not necessarily non-Christian. He concludes that the church-sect continuum should not include the cult because the cult is the first stage in the formation of a new religion, and that all founded religions can be seen to have developed originally from cults.

This analysis seems somewhat contradictory, since a macro-view of the secularisation process as routinisation would encompass the cultic origins of any religious form. However, since most discussions of the nature of the cults display ambivalence and ambiguity in conceptualisation and analytical application it will suffice to say that there need be no necessary process of secularisation which starts from the routinisation of the charisma of the cult (Wallis, 1974).

Evidence for this view is provided by Jackson and Jobling (1968) who suggest that there are two analytically distinct, but dynamically related, concepts of cult – the mystic-religious, and the quasi-religious. The former conceives of the wider society as irrelevant, while the latter is world-affirming and instrumental. Hence the extreme of 'other-worldliness', it is suggested, does not exhaust the range of cultic experience.

The preceding analysis has shown how religion, when identified with its organisational manifestations becomes prone to conceptualisation in terms of conventional usage. This identification of religion with its specific historical categories appears to be rarely made explicit. Certainly, the variety of discussions of secularisation, which at some stage involve such concepts as church or sect, seems to indicate at least some extension of usage to contemporary society from some 'Utopian' ideal, if not total unrelatedness.

However, such usage need not be ideological as well, although the common identification between contemporary pluralism and the end of the secularisation process may raise some doubts. The main conclusions to be drawn seem to be that the openings for myth-making in this area are great, so long as notions such as church, sect, cult etc. are as culture-bound as they appear at present. Werner Cohn (1969) has warned of the problems of defining religion for cultures which stand outside the Judaeo-Christian tradition. However, such problems are not quite so acute in the case of Japan, where sectarianism appears to exist on a similar level to Western society. Thus Wilson can say:

> the Japanese sects draw on various divergent traditions – Buddhism, Shinto and occasionally Christianity for their teachings, western organisational ideas for their structure, and sometimes modern international ideologies for their programme . . . (Wilson, 1970:219).

Care must be taken not to extend historically-rooted conventional categories of religious organisation beyond their temporal and spatial co-ordinates without a strong theoretical underpinning. To do so may lead to the construction of a social myth.

Conclusion

This chapter has been concerned with exploring the ways in which empirical material about change in religion has become generalised into a social myth. It has suggested that the three criteria isolated by Toulmin for identifying the myth-making process can be translated into three fundamental methodological errors, exhibited to a greater or lesser degree by the secularisation processes analysed. These three, the errors of idealisation, permeation and categorisation, all stem from the uncritical acceptance of the premises that there really was a time when man and society were completely religious, that their religiosity was homogeneously distributed within the social framework, and that common-sense definitions of religion in Western culture (inevitably linked with religion's institutional forms) are adequate bases for producing a theoretical model of the secularisation process.

In the first instance, evidence was produced to suggest that the idealisations of social scientists can and do intrude (generally for implicit ideological reasons) into their analyses of the 'base-line' society from which change was said to occur. In addition, it was suggested that religion does not permeate evenly through the social structure, but will affect its various elements differentially, so that no single process of change need necessarily occur at any one period of time. It was also noted that, certainly within Western culture, the dominant mode of 'being religious' was invariably associated with the institutions of Christianity, specifically within the ambit of the church-sect analyses.

Hence, in conclusion, it is necessary to accept that the major 'theories' of the secularisation process have incorrectly generalised from their empirical material. This 'systematic empiricism' is of only limited value for the sociological theorist trying to explain the processes of change under discussion. The evidence for the development of a social myth of secularisation seems to be well founded. However, the empirical and methodological critiques do not suggest how the problem can best be approached, nor how the term secularisation can be rescued, assuming that it has some remaining utility, perhaps for the purposes of social engineering. The next chapter attempts to develop a theoretical model of the 'religious' in order to provide secularisation with a theoretically legitimated role in the sociological framework for the study of religion and change.

4 The theoretical critique

In the previous discussions it has been assumed, for the most part, that indices of change in the character of religious institutions in society, as well as in the institutions themselves, are directly available in their other dimensions. This reductionist approach has an element of truth; certainly it is true to say that institutions are made up of organisations, which, in their turn, are derived from collections of individual social roles. However this does not deny the autonomy of each sector.

The possibility of changes independent of changes in other parts of the chain tends to be overlooked. Hence the notion that, for example, religious institutions can be made up of both religious and non-religious organisations (depending upon the definition of religion used), or that religious and non-religious roles are to be found in religious organisations is often ignored.[1] Similarly, discussions of the religious in non-religious organisations or institutions is also bypassed, or bogged down in the conceptual fog of functional alternatives (with notable exceptions, e.g. Luckmann, 1967).

However, such conceptions have been available in sociology since its inception. For example, Simmel has noted:

> Social groups which are the most diverse imaginable in purpose and general significance, may nevertheless show identical forms of behaviour towards one another on the part of their individual members. . . . However diverse the interests are that give rise to these sociations the *forms* in which interests are realised may yet be identical. . . . The religious contents of life although they remain identical, sometimes demand an unregulated, sometimes a centralised, form of community (Simmel, 1950:22).

It will be suggested here that a clearer sociological understanding of the process of secularisation can be derived from the distinction made by, among others, Durkheim, Weber and Simmel between *religion* and the *religious*.[2] That is, an attempt will be made to show why there is a necessary difference and autonomy between the level of personal relations and organisational or institutional structures. This distinction was not made with any degree of clarity in the three writers mentioned, and hence the first part of the discussion will be of an expository nature. In the second part the relationship between this distinction and a sociological conception of the secularisation process will be attempted by emphasising the need to understand the necessary ubiquity of the religious within social relations, while accepting the possibility of its absence on the organisational or institutional level. No attempt will be made to differentiate in detail between the institutional and organisational levels for the purposes of this discussion. The outcome will be in the form of a paradigm for the process of secularisation.

A theory of the religious

Much has been written concerning the similarities between Weber's concept of charisma and Durkheim's notion of the sacred. This has generally overlooked the essential similarities between charisma and the sacred, and Simmel's discussion of the forms of religious social relationship exemplified in the concept of 'piety'.

Discussions, such as those found in Parsons (1937) and Nisbet (1970), concentrate upon the ends of the social relationships involved rather than the social relationships themselves. As a result, the attempts to identify charisma with sacred (in the case of Parsons and Nisbet) and both with piety (in the case of Nisbet) are unsatisfactory, and lead both authors to seek justification for their approaches in terms of the writers' differing aims. Parsons sees Weber as providing a further extension and application of areas which Durkheim failed to develop. Nisbet differentiates between them in terms of social and individual origins, while comparing them with Simmel in terms of the role of the religious impulse.

What is suggested here is that no such justifications are required. The three analyses are more closely comparable than has been assumed heretofore.

The focus of the discussion will be upon the concept of the religious as describing the specific form of the social relationship to be found within the undifferentiated group. Piety will be seen as providing the prime example of this form, the objects of which can be described as charismatic or sacred. Hence the discussion

101

will constitute a plea for a return to the Founding Fathers whose work in this field would appear to have been misunderstood or overlooked, and will follow Nisbet's account in its initial stages.

Durkheim (1915) is concerned primarily with analysing the most fundamental dichotomy in social life: the distinction between the sacred and the profane. It is an absolute distinction and a universal one, though things can move from one sphere to the other. Like his concept of contract, the sacred, for Durkheim, derives ultimately from the community.

The sources of obligation, and hence the source of all authority, is in the *conscience collective,* whose ways are *sui generis,* and hence mysterious. Things which are mysterious, and thus emanate from the collective mind, are sacred, while those constructed by the individual on a personal basis are profane. Religious ideas are collective ideas representing collective realities, and based on a division of the world into the sacred and the profane. Religious rites are manifestations of the integrated nature of the group. Using Australian aborigines as an example, Durkheim underlines this point:

> When the Australians, scattered in little groups, spend their time in hunting and fishing, they lose sight of what concerns their clan or tribe; their only thought is to catch as many game as possible. On feast days, on the contrary, these preoccupations are necessarily eclipsed; being essentially profane they are excluded from these sacred periods. At this time their thoughts are centred upon their common beliefs, their common traditions, the memory of their great ancestors, the collective idea of which they are the incarnation; in a word, upon social things (1915: 348–9).

Hence, for Durkheim, relations with the sacred, that is *religious* social relations, are not necessarily continuously present in daily life.[3] They represent specific examples of social behaviour in close knit communal situations. Sacred things, 'that is to say things set apart and forbidden', are in Durkheim's definition the objects of a 'united system of beliefs and practices' that can best be described as a religion. But the major significance comes, not from this fact, but from the uniting power of the beliefs and practices in the formation of moral communities, or churches.

The vital element in this conception is the form of social relationships involved, and not just their ends. Durkheim is not so much concerned with the sacred as with the *quality* of the social relationships themselves. The essence of the individual's relationship with the sacred is that of intimacy. Durkheim, when talking of the doubts which arise in individuals' minds concerning the authenticity of the sacred, and how these are overcome when the common faith is reanimated through group unity, notes that:

> After it has been restored, it easily triumphs over all the private doubts that may have arisen in individual minds ... In spite of their apparent failure, men can no longer believe that the gods will die, because they feel them *living in their own hearts* (1915: 346; my emphasis).

The concept of the community, and the specific forms of social relationship to be found within it, are explored in greater detail by Durkheim (1933) in his study of the division of labour. In this study he distinguishes between two forms of social solidarity: the mechanical and the organic. Under mechanical solidarity, the individual is bound *directly* to the group without any intermediary. The society is a 'more or less organised totality of beliefs and sentiments common to all the members of the group'. Within organic society, on the other hand, the individual relates to the *parts* which compose society. Society is a 'system of different, special functions, which definite relations unite'. This is an analytical distinction since, according to Durkheim (1933: 129ff), both types exist as 'two aspects of one and the same reality'.

The significance of this distinction for the preceding discussion lies in its characterisation of the ties of mechanical solidarity as being based on intimacy, and as being, therefore, essentially religious in nature.

It is suggested, therefore, that the specific form of religious social relationships is to be found in mechanical forms of social solidarity.[4] Hence to suggest that the sacred is the same as the social, and that Durkheim's analysis is simplistic as a result, is to overlook the subtlety of his approach. The identification is not with the social, but with the *form* of the social, characterised by an intimate relationship.

The relationship which exists between Weber's notion of charisma and Durkheim's concept of the sacred, is noted by Parsons in his introduction to Weber's *Sociology of Religion* (1963). His analysis, in the *Structure of Social Action,* is closely followed by Nisbet (1970: 252). In fact, Nisbet goes so far as to suggest that charismatic is synonymous with sacred-endowing. In its individual sense, charisma is a

> certain quality of an individual personality by which he is set apart from ordinary men and treated as endowed with

supernatural, superhuman, or at least specifically exceptional powers or qualities (Weber, 1964:358).

It may be manifested in a very wide variety of types of individuals ranging from shamans to intellectuals.

Recognition of charismatic quality 'is a matter of complete personal devotion to the possessor of the quality'. The group which follows the charismatic leader has no divisions into spheres of authority, or privilege, nor competence. It is based on 'an emotional form of communal relationship', and charismatic authority is therefore 'specifically outside the realm of everyday routine and the profane sphere'. In this pure form, charismatic authority only exists 'in the process of originating'.

It should be noted that both Parsons and Nisbet see Weber as having generalised the concept of charisma so that it adheres as much to things as to people. Routinisation involves a transfer from the personal which leads to

> hereditary incorporation into families, offices, castes, races and communities; even, one is justified in saying, into things . . . to which charisma has been attached by its place in some momentous event in life of a divine or deeply revered leader (Nisbet, 1970:252).

It also means a move to either traditional or rational-legal everyday authority. What changes, therefore, is

> not the quality of the charisma as such but its concrete mode of embodiment and its relation to other elements of the particular concrete complex (Parsons, 1937:665).

Parsons, unlike Nisbet, concentrates more on the significance of social relationships in his comparison of Weber and Durkheim. He notes, for example, that charisma in primitive religion is correlated with a specific sense of the world of supernatural entities, which 'is nothing but the ideological correlate of the attitude of respect', and further that 'the religious elements of action are concerned with men's relations to supernatural entities'.

Charisma is a wider concept than it first appears, since the supernatural entities are inseparably linked with ultimate concerns and problems of meaning. What is to be seen as important lies in the specific relationships between individuals and the charismatic authority, which recognise the special quality of the charisma. Parsons suggests, in conclusion, that charisma and the sacred are the bases of legitimacy and moral authority in Weber and Durkheim.

Nisbet's identification of the sacred with charisma leads him to conclude that the origins of the former, in collective society, differ from those of the latter, which are personal. Parsons, at least, recognises the necessary communal nature of both forms of the non-profane aspects of the world, but does not explore the underlying reasons. Weber's charismatic authority, however, is only seen as charismatic through the recognition of its quality as manifested by the disciples of the charismatic leader. Similarly, even when routinised, the charismatic quality of the office or object is recognisable only through social action.

It is the specific form of the social relationships involved that singles out an individual, thing or abstract concept as bearing the gift of grace. Hence the parallel with Durkheim's analysis. Both writers grasped the centrality of the idea of the religious as a form of social relationship between the individual and the group, constituted as a moral community and unified by a common recognition of the sacred as manifested in the quality of charisma.

Thus, for Weber, the underlying importance of the role of charisma rests on the personal devotion exhibited by the individual to the possessor of that charisma. In its original form, this devotion is to be found in the undifferentiated community of like-minded followers; the parallel with Durkheim's concept of mechanical solidarity needs to be pursued no further. Weber, like Durkheim, is principally concerned to elucidate the social relationship which has been described as religious, and it is suggested that a necessary and logical extension can be made to his analysis in order to complete this elucidation.

Weber recognised the transitory nature of the original form of charismatic authority. He also saw that this nature would be destroyed by the process of routinisation. However, he did not suggest, as is suggested here, that the form of the social relationship need not necessarily change with routinisation. In fact, the form of social relationship cannot change if the routinised object (whether human or not) retains its charismatic quality, since recognition of the existence of this quality stems from social action.

It is possible, therefore, to suggest that the religious may not be manifested as widely within the group surrounding the charismatic object after routinisation, but that each member must (at some time) subscribe to or undergo the religious form of social relationship with it. In Durkheim's terms, members of the routinised group may be related in terms of organic solidarity; but, in order to maintain the charismatic qualities of the object of the group and possibly the group itself, they need to participate in some way in a relationship of mechanical solidarity.

This relationship does not involve participation by all the mem-

105

H

bers of the group at the same time. It is possible that only a specific individual and the charismatic object are required, and so long as the members of the group always subscribe to the vesting of charisma in that object, then they can *experience* the religious relationship as often or as little as they want.

Simmel's (1957, 1959) contributions to the sociology of religion have been strangely neglected by most of the major writers in the field. This is unfortunate, it will be argued, since his insights into the meaning of the religious provide the key to understanding the similarities between his work and that of Weber and Durkheim. This understanding is rooted in the idea of *faith* as the central binding element of society.

Simmel does not feel that the manifestations of *religion* exhaust the possibilities for the existence of religious feelings or impulses. Religion provides the extreme development and differentiation as an independent content of life. The religious is to be found in many places. It is a 'cooperating element in various situations'.[5] He argues that religion can be seen as a highly, and independently, differentiated form of human relationship. The description of the religious stems, not from looking at existing religions, but rather from a specific form of interaction.

Many human relations, notes Simmel, comprise a religious element, including those between a patriot and his country, or a devoted child and his parent, or the soldier and his army. The religious element is, variously,

a peculiar admixture of unselfish surrender and fervent desire, of humility and exaltation, of sensual concreteness and spiritual abstraction, which occasions a certain degree of emotional tension, a specific ardour and a certainty of subjective conditions, an inclusion of the subject experiencing them in a high order – an order which is at the same time felt to be something subjective and personal (1957).

The religious forms can vary in intensity; relationships need not be religious in character at all times. The relation of the individual to the group is best described as religious in this sense, that is to say including 'exaltation, devotion and fervency'. It is from these that the ideas of gods or 'ideal contents' are developed as an attempt to protect and substain them. Religion arises, therefore, from the special feelings found in the group and, once developed, acts reciprocally upon it, effecting the 'direct psychical relations of men among themselves', and resulting in the 'now well known, and recalled original, quality of *religiosity*'.

Simmel also suggests that belief in God or a similar supernatural entity, involves a subjective relationship best described as a 'going out of affection'. The parallel is with all human relationships, which are based on faith to some degree, as noted earlier. Without faith, society would disintegrate.

It is from the subjective process that religion, an object for that faith, develops. Once independent, it spontaneously authenticates itself from within,

> just as it is no rare phenomenon for a certain object to produce
> a certain psychical process in us, and afterwards for this process,
> having become independent, to create a corresponding object
> for itself (1957:337).

Hence any objects can become the objects of faith.

Another important aspect of groups is the need to produce a unity or nomos from the chaos of nature. The 'highest representation' of this, says Simmel, is to be found in the idea of the divine. But the very fact that all social life is a relationship necessarily defines it as a unity.

The group which forms a religion allows the energies of the individual members to be fully developed without the disturbing effects of competition. The common goal is achievable in principle without mutual exclusion, and may even be achieved only through co-operation. Religion, like the state, is an abstract concept, external to the group and unifying it. What is important in this parallel is the uniformity of the various social relations of individuals subsumed under the concept.

> I call attention to the feeling of dependence, in which the
> essence of all religion has been found. The individual feels
> himself bound to a universal, to something higher, out of
> which he came, and into which he will return, and from which
> he expects assistance and salvation, from which he differs and
> is yet identical with it (1957:341).

Simmel (1959:24) identifies the 'strange mixture of selfless devotion and desires, of humility and elation, of sensual immediacy and spiritual abstraction' as the concept of piety. Nisbet, at this point, notes that there are men who are pious without reference to God; they endow non-religious objects or relationships with a religious character. 'They are religious natures without a religion.' This observation underlines the similarity between Simmel and Weber's discussion of charismatic authority.

Simmel, therefore, sees the specific forms of social relationship which he describes as religious, as based on the faith which binds all group relationships. However, by their special nature, not every

107

social relationship within groups can be described as religious, since it does not necessarily involve the concept of piety. The religious relation is identified by feelings of dependence and unity; it is also identified by emotional strength and interdependence.

It is this form of social relationship which Simmel (Wolff, 1950) discusses in his analysis of the dyad. The dyad exists only when the two members of the group agree that it should. Either member is able, therefore, to affect its survival in the knowledge that, without the other, the group will collapse. Such a relationship between members of the dyadic group makes for constraint, intensity, closeness and intimacy. In reality, it is characterised by the most extreme form of faith. Potentially the dyadic relationship is the most religious. As Simmel himself notes, the unity of social life is such that 'the fate of each is felt by all' (1957:338). This is nowhere more true than in the dyadic group.

However, as noted above, not all social relations need be religious in character at all times. The same is true in dyadic group relations, where the notion of triviality is introduced by Simmel to describe situations when the specific sense of individual uniqueness between participants, or the recognition of the permanence of the supra-individual societal unit, does not arise. Religious relations can be seen as trivial, in this sense, for much of the time. The comparison here is with Durkheim's analysis of the nature of relations with the sacred, and Weber's concept of charismatic quality in its routin-ised sense.

Relationships need not remain dyadic, but can become triadic in character. The triad presents itself to each of its members as having an existence independent of his particular will, and its existence is not threatened by the withdrawal of one member. Hence there is greater freedom, but less intensity and affectivity. But it may be that relationships within the triad are in fact dyadic in nature; that individual members confront the group as a single entity, and vice versa (Rustin, 1971). Here the parallel between dyadic and triadic relations and mechanical and organic solidarity may be of value. In mechanical solidarity the individual relates to the group in a dyadic manner; he is seen as essential to its survival. Thus, after all, part of the function of repressive law rests in the fact that offences are seen as offences against the *group as a whole*.

In this way it is possible to link Simmel's work more closely with that of Weber and Durkheim through his discussion of the social relationships involved in piety. These social relations, which have been described as religious, are found in situations of mechani-cal solidarity, original charismatic authority and dyadic group re-lations. In all three cases the form of the relationship has been divorced from the form of the group which may or may not necessarily be a religion.

It can be argued that this would make the relationships between children and their parents religious in character. But contemporary parenthood is based more on notions of equal partnership than of authority or mystery. These elements more accurately typify relations between Victorian children and their parents. Certainly parental attitudes in that era seemed grounded in religious authority which had an almost sacred character.

A paradigm for the process of secularisation

The notion of the religious as a specific form of social relationship found within the undifferentiated group context provides the clue to understanding the different uses of religion, and hence secularisation. In an undifferentiated society (the discussion now moves to ideal-typical terms) the institutional and organisational aspects of religion are not present. In this sense, undifferentiated society provides the only example of a society that is 'really religious'. and move along the continuum involving increasing social differentiation can therefore be described as secularisation in the sense that society ceases to be 'really religious'. This, however, seems a rather shallow conceptualisation.

In more differentiated societies, the institutional and organisational religious forms separate out into religions. However, these religions, as has been shown already, need not be continuously supported by the notion of the religious. Similarly the notion of the religious may be present in those institutional and organisational areas which are not specifically described as religions. This obviates the necessity of identifying the 'really religious' as the basepoint for the process of secularisation. It is necessary to recognise that such a process will be related to the institutional or organisational levels, and not to the level of interpersonal relationships. Hence the misguided notions of, for example, the disappearance of the religious in modern society, can be dispensed with. Secularisation should say nothing about this level of analysis.

The problem of functional definitions of religion and secularisation is also solved. It is no longer necessary to entertain such concepts as functional alternatives because all institutions and organisations will in some sense be describable as *religious* even though they may not be *religions*. Similarly the difficulty of identifying the religious nature of non-Western religions is overcome when this distinction is remembered. Thus the sociologist is able to work more easily with the concepts of religion and secularisation by framing his discussions within the organisational or institutional order.

It is now possible to bring back the notion of content and to use it as the basis for *classifying* the institutional and organisational order. Similarly notions of the religious can be related to the content of religions, in order to characterise the religious experience as accepted by a conventional usage. That is to say that the religious forms of social relationships may be linked with specific notions of religion rooted in the historical context. A complete sociological account of religion would necessarily have to include both aspects. However, it would also have to include those experiences which fall outside the conventionally defined sphere of religion, and this is possible only so long as the necessary distinction, between religion and the religious, as outlined above, is borne in mind.

In Christianity it is possible to imagine that the majority of social relations among individuals who form a church are of a secondary nature. Some, however, will be primary and, of these, only a few can be described as religious: the individual's relations with God; or perhaps his relationship with the minister during communion. However, such relations are usually not continuous, and probably cease when the individual leaves the service. The quality and the quantity of such relationships within the church would be difficult to determine, and such an exercise may be of little value if the 'intimacy' involved is capable of reproduction at any time. Thus, a religious relationship with God on the part of a member of the church need not necessitate his entering a church. He may be in almost continuous state of intimacy with his God while at work, or at home.

The term secularisation would not, therefore, appear to be very useful in describing changes in the *religious*. The religious, as a social relationship, will be either present or absent. Certainly, the notion of process, which is implied by secularisation, is inappropriate when discussing the religious. The first element in any paradigm, therefore, must distinguish between religion and the religious.

The specification of different levels of analysis becomes important as a result. If the religious is available independently of the organisation involved, then perhaps that organisation may become secularised even though composed of individuals whose primary social relationships are religious. This may be also true on the cultural level. However it is not enough, in order to describe the culture as becoming secularised, to say that various aspects of religious organisation have declined. The correlations may be high, but no logical relationship exists. This will have implications for the entire range of cross-cultural analyses, and limit comparisons between historical periods within the same society. The same aspects of the same level of analysis need to be compared before any judgment can be made.

The second element in a paradigm indicates, therefore, at least three levels of analysis: the cultural, concerned with both the normative aspects of society and the institutions which transmit those norms; the organisational, describing the structural manifestations of these institutions; and the interpersonal, relating individual behaviour patterns to the organisations. This latter level is reserved for the religious, and religion is then used to describe an organisation or an institution.

The third element in a secularisation paradigm will stem from the organisational and cultural levels of analysis. It will distinguish between definitions of religion which are exclusive, and those which are inclusive (see Robertson, 1970: chapter 3). Such a distinction has no utility on the interpersonal level since the religious may be manifest in *any* situation which allows the individual to form a social relationship with another individual, or with a group (such as the Church of England), or with an abstract idea (such as Tao, Nirvana or God).

An inclusive definition, such as that suggested by Durkheim, could allow conventionally defined secular organisations such as football supporters' clubs, or institutions such as Communism, to be classified as religions. Exclusive definitions which often base their distinctions on either the goals or the objects of the movement, are more likely to fit into conventionally defined categories. Most accepted religions are concerned with salvation and have supernatural entities as their objects of worship.

However, the differences between exclusive and inclusive definitions of religion have other implications for the study of secularisation. Robertson (1970:38) notes that an inclusive definition is generally nominal and often functional, while an exclusive one is real and substantive. He suggests that the 'epitome of the nominal, functional approach to religion' is best illustrated by the notion that all societies manifest religious beliefs and values. The utility of a concept of secularisation under such conditions is obviously questionable, since even though the form may change, religiosity is necessarily still present. It is suggested, therefore, that the term be restricted to analyses of religion based on exclusive definitions.

The next element in the paradigm relates the variety of processes which pass for secularisation in the literature to the sociological use of the term itself, as discussed in preceding chapters. These processes have originally been used to explain secularisation in specific situations. They are severely limited in their application both in space and in time. In fact much of what passes for discussion of the secularisation process is based upon extensions or distortion of these original processes. However, each such process is valid and useful within its context and open to rigorous replication. Together with others it can be collected to form a *pattern* of secularisation which is best understood as a *generic* term, subsuming particular processes. It indicates a decline or decrease in the importance, significance and salience of religion at a specified level of analysis, over a specific period of time. Such changes would occur in either or both of the two levels already indicated, namely the organisational and the cultural. The particular analyses would be based upon religion defined in real and substantive terms.

In effect, this suggests a taxonomy of secularisation processes, each useful within its own limitations. The taxonomy will be constructed according to the main variables used by each specific analysis. Thus secularisation can be seen as the result of declining membership or attendance figures, as well as an increasing number of bureaucratically structured organisations. This allows the general process to include specific analyses which appear contradictory on the surface, and in the case of the decline of religion and its increasing pluralisation.

The main purpose of this taxonomy is to allow the construction of a *profile* of the state of religion within a society at a given time and on a given level. This profile will indicate changes which have occurred within different variables, assuming that the comparisons have been made with the same point in the past. Hence the generic term secularisation can be used to describe a societal profile in which all the particular indicators, shown by the various processes, are unidirectional and show positive changes to have occurred. It is not to be expected that the correlation between all processes will be high, nor that it will even be positive. The profile will indicate a general trend in certain areas, the choice of which area depending upon the investigator.

Any society may be high on several measures of secularisation but medium or low on others. Church and state, for example, may be constitutionally separated and religion excluded from major institutions such as education; there may even be a proliferation of religious groups; but, as in the USA, membership attendance figures may be high. In the United Kingdom, the Queen is still the Head of the Church; religion is still taught in schools by law, but membership and attendance figures are low. In Japan, religious groups proliferate; membership and attendance figures are high; but church and state are constitutionally separate.

These profiles on the organisational level are possible on the cultural level as well, and a secularisation profile of a particular culture can be constructed in much the same way. Throughout this analysis, however, it should be remembered that nothing is said, nor indeed can be, about the religious, which may or may not be present at either the organisational or institutional levels.

Finally, it may be possible to use secularisation to describe the overall state of religion in society by combining the secularisation profiles at the organisational and institutional levels. This would not be possible, as noted earlier, through simple aggregation, because the two levels are logically distinct. However, it may be possible when the two profiles correlate highly. This would allow comparison *between* societies, as well as *within* societies, and overcome some of the difficulties involved in cross-cultural studies of religion.

The paradigm for secularisation can, therefore, be summarised in the following manner:

1 There is a distinction to be made between religion and the religious.
2 There are at least three levels of analysis – the interpersonal, the organisational and the cultural.
3 The religious is available at all levels, but because of its nature cannot become secularised.
4 Religion can be defined inclusively or exclusively.
5 Secularisation is not useful when religion is inclusively defined.
6 With exclusive definitions, secularisation is best seen as a generic term.
7 The generic term subsumes a variety of particular processes. These are limited in level of analysis, in time and in space.
8 Indicators of processes provide a secularisation profile.
9 High correlation between secularisation profiles at the organisational and cultural levels allow the generic terms to describe changes in religion at the societal level.

In conclusion, a paradigm can be constructed in which the process of secularisation is seen to be sociologically useful as a *generic* term subsuming a variety of particular processes, limited in space and time as well as level of analysis. It is suggested that a secularisation profile can be constructed:

(a) by some process of aggregation on each level, and

(b) when profiles of a similar level correlate highly.

The profile allows the use of secularisation as a term describing society as a whole or the organisations and institutions within it. The possible presence of the religious is assumed to be independent, to a large extent, of any degree of secularisation.

The paradigm is rooted within a *theoretical* model of the religious, which provides it with a rational and coherent justification. The role of secularisation as a sociological concept is thus given a specific and logical meaning, and is not subject to the vagaries of *ad hoc* empiricism which have bedevilled its use until now, and prompted sociologists like Martin (1969b) to dispense with its use in sociology altogether.

Secularisation, exploration and social engineering

The theoretical problematic has suggested a specific use for the term secularisation. It has a role, within a broad paradigmatic structure, as a generic term subsuming a variety of specific analyses of change in the religious sphere. In effect, its usefulness lies in its ordering power as part of a more general taxonomy to describe one of a variety of processes of change in society. The emphasis is not on the explanation of change but on its classification. The laws developed, as Braithwaite (1953) notes, may be 'merely generalisations involved in classifying things into various classes'.

Hence, the major stumbling block in using the concept of secularisation in sociology is removed with the recognition that, in itself, it is not a theoretical term even though it is a by-product of a theoretical model.

The question then remains: what role *can* it play? Bearing in mind the Willers' warning on the limitation of systematic empiricism (1973:137), it is still possible to delineate two major roles. First, there is an *exploratory* role, which allows the sociologist to develop a fairly complex taxonomy for any particular social structure in order to direct future research into areas which may not intuitively appear important. This is a fairly major task and beyond the scope of this analysis. Thus, in Britain for example, the aspect of secularisation labelled decline in the taxonomy is extremely well documented in the work of Wilson, Martin, etc. More work, however, is obviously required in the area of the generalisation thesis where only Towler (1974) seems to have made any real impact. This exploratory exercise can be elaborated for all the elements in the taxonomy and, when the research is complete in the main, the outlines of the secularisation 'profile' for Britain can be tentatively drawn.

The second main role that suggests itself is that of *social engineering*. Quite obviously, many of the elements in the secularisation paradigm have far-reaching effects on the broader social structure, especially for the contemporary parish and the role of the ministry. The planning implications have not been seriously explored by any writers in Britain. This role is necessarily a very limited one, specific

114

in both time and space, as well as scope. However, the development of a secularisation profile based on the taxonomy is probably the best way of ensuring that the wider implications of policy changes are explored.

In conclusion, it can readily be seen that the term secularisation can have a role to play in sociology, although a very different one from that outlined in the existing literature. By using it in this way, and recognising the specificity of the many analyses of change that make up the paradigm, it is possible to rescue the term from the process of mythification.

Conclusion

An attempt has been made to provide a sociological critique of some of the major theories of the secularisation process. It has used the notion of social myth as a basis, developing Toulmin's analysis of scientific myths. A social myth adapts or extends particular analyses, sometimes for ideological purposes, beyond their limitations of scope in order to make broad judgments which they are able to uphold in themselves.

The process of secularisation has been criticised for subsuming a great variety of often contradictory analyses which have been altered in this myth-making way in order to give the term a spurious validity. Such criticisms, for this very reason, have gone so far as to suggest that secularisation no longer be accepted as a sociological concept. This discussion, on the other hand, has provided a sociological critique by exploring its various uses, but does not suggest that the term be jettisoned prematurely. In order to do this, it has approached the mythification process on both the substantive and the methodological levels, providing evidence to show that the specific analyses (or major theories) have formed the basis for a social myth of secularisation. Examples have been drawn, as far as possible, from societies which have industrialisation as a common independent variable, for example, Great Britain, the USA and Japan, which also provide different religious traditions. In Britain religion appears to be of little importance, while in the USA it is considered an almost essential part of being American. In Japan it is all-pervasive, with organisations having a total membership in excess of the Japanese population. Japan also provides an example outside the Judaeo-Christian tradition.

The first main section of the investigation analysed the substantive aspects of the major theories of secularisation. They were classified according to the definitions of religion upon which the theories were based, and fell into three categories: primarily institutional, primarily normative and primarily cognitive. At least one process was taken from each category and explored in some detail. Generally, the conclusions suggested that the ideological nature of many of the studies was rooted in the view that the most secular form of society was contemporary society. The extensions from particular investigations, or their offered interpretations, were in the direction of continued progress toward some rational secular norm. It was also noted that the usual interpretation of the term secularisation within sociological theory had a number of underpinning 'logics' which bore only distant relationships to it. These, too, it was suggested, had attained mythical status.

In all cases, it was found that a major source of error lay in the uncritical use of conventional definitions of religion and religiosity. This formed the basis of the methodological investigations in the second section of the discussion. The three criteria suggested by Toulmin for identifying the presence of social myths were found to coincide with the three main assumptions behind the concept of secularisation: namely that there was a period when man and/or society was 'really religious'; that the impact of religion on society is uniformly distributed throughout that society: and that religion can be identified with the organisational and institutional forms current within contemporary society or drawn from its history. In all cases, these asumptions were found to raise secularisation to the status of a social myth.

This discussion has, therefore, been an attack on contemporary sociology in several ways; it has suggested the ubiquity of the ideology of progress in sociologists' views of the place of religion in society; it has argued that this ideology has been promoted through the use of a particular methodology; it has suggested that a major ordering concept, secularisation, has become a sociological myth (and that, by implication, it may not be alone); and finally it has suggested that there is little by way of scientific theory to help conceptualise the understanding of the secularisation process.

Barry Hindess (1973) has stated this last point most clearly, with references to generalisations made on the basis of the use of 'official statistics', when he notes:

> The usefulness of such statistics is a function of the theoretical problematic in which they are to be used and on the uses to which they may be put within it (1973:45).

He argues that statistics fall prey to at least two major misapprehensions: that cases can be unambiguously defined; and that the defining agencies do so unambiguously anyway. Using examples

116

such as social class in India, and doctors' definitions of death, he makes a convincing case for the necessity of developing a *theoretical* problematic within which to couch sociological explanation.

The 'theories' of the secularisation process discussed above have, in all cases, been based upon empirical generalisations, not theoretical (scientific) systems. As Willer and Willer point out:

> Scientific theory is concerned with concepts, terms not defined by reference to observation, which consequently enter into exact theoretical relations with one another which are often expressed mathematically. The 'theoretical' empiricism practiced in sociology is characterised by the deliberate use of observationally defined empirical categories which cannot be related by any theoretical means, including mathematical connectives (1973:3).

Hence 'theories' of the secularisation process become social myths through their reliance upon systematic empiricism. These 'theories' use concepts rooted in the language of sources, folk typifications which bear only accidental relationships to any truly theoretical system or problematic. These *generalisations* of the secularisation process have been based, using an altered version of Aron's (1964:30) famous phrase, upon comparisons between contemporary society and some societies in the historical past which have, as their only common feature, the fact that they are neither modern nor secular.

The main danger awaiting the sociologist of secularisation, apart from not having a theory or a paradigm, appears to be the ease with which he can create a social myth of the secularisation process. This will still hold true if his main concern is with one of the particular processes. As Robertson notes:

> if the analysis is accurate in pinning down a firm, inexorable series of secularisation processes and showing how sociology itself may be contributing to these, we must still be extremely wary about attributing too much significance to the present. *Presentism*, that posture which tends to claim the uniqueness of the modern period, clouds our judgement as to the long-drawn-out historical unfolding of changes we diagnose in the modern world, and also persuades us that the changes we see are inevitably coming to some early point of termination or fruition (1970:240).

It has been suggested that just such a posture has been a major factor in the creation of the secularisation myth.

The preceding chapter began with an attempt to develop a

theoretical system from the work of Weber, Durkheim and Simmel. It focused specifically on the concept of the religious as a basis for understanding the relationship between being religious and being a member of a religion. In a sense, it asked the 'wrong' questions as far as the traditional secularisation processes are concerned, but by doing so highlighted, in a *theoretical* manner, the specific weaknesses of working wholly within an empiricist problematic, using the methodology of generalisation developed by systematic empiricist sociology.

Notes

Chapter 1 Introduction: Social and scientific myths

1 It should be made clear at this point that a structuralist definition of myth (e.g., Lévi-Strauss, 1963) is not being developed.
2 Robertson (1970) provides an interesting exposition of the various relationships to be found between sociologists, and, for example, secularisation, which underlines this point.

Chapter 2 Processes of secularisation

1 See Landis (1961). A good summary may be found in E. S. Goustad, 'America's Institutions of Faith' in Cutler (1968).
2 For bibliography see: C. Y. Glock, 'The Sociology of Religion' in Merton, Broom and Cottrell (1959); Paul Hoenigsheim, 'Sociology of Religion – Complementary Analysis of Religious Institutions' in Becker and Boskoff (1957); C. L. Hunt, 'The Sociology of Religion' in Roucek (1959); L. Schneider, 'Some Problems in the Sociology of Religion' in Faris (1968).
3 For France see: 'French "sociologie religieuse"' in Boulard (1960), and Le Bras et al. (1966). For German bibliography see Goldschmidt (1962) and Matthes (1962). A review of much of the European material can be found in Fogarty (1957), chapter XXII: 340–57. See also relevant sections in Mol (1972). For Japan see *Journal of Asian and African Studies* (vol. III), nos 1 and 2, January–April 1968, special double issue on the sociology of Japanese religion (edited by K. Ishwaran), and for the place of folk religion in traditional Japan see Ichiro (1968) and Morioka (1970). A good discussion of the place of the 'new religions' can be found in McFarland (1967) and Thomsen (1963). See also Morioka, 'Contemporary Changes in Japanese Religions' in Birnbaum and Lenzer (1969) and Norbeck (1970).
4 Wilson (1966). See also McIntyre (1967) and Martin (1969b), esp. section 1. A broad critical review of the literature on religion in England, including surveys of attitudes and beliefs, can be found in Martin (1967). For Scotland, see Highet (1950, 1960). See also their

articles in Mol (1972). Other material is available in D. A. Martin (ed.), *A Sociological Yearbook of Religion in Britain*, vol. 1 (1968 ff) (SCM Press), which is now edited by M. Hill; and R. Currie and A. Gilbert, 'Religion' in Halsey (1972).

5 See Yang (1970), chapter 12 for general applicability outside the Judaeo–Christian tradition of this concept.

6 See Nelson (1968, 1969). See also von Wiese (1932) and W. E. Mann, *Sect, Cult and Church in Alberta* quoted in Yinger (1971:279).

7 T. Parsons, 'Christianity and Modern Industrial Society' in Tiryakian (1963). For an earlier discussion which covers much the same ground, see Smith (1894). The general underlying principles are to be found in Durkheim (1933).

8 See C. Becker (1932), Hazard (1954) and Cassirer (1951) for general discussions of the impact of Enlightenment thought on religious domination in most areas of society. For a discussion of the disengagement of science see Butterfield (1957) and Feuer (1965).

9 Note the contrast with Wilson (1966), who regards the sects as evidence *for* secularisation. This is indicative of some of the misunderstandings aroused by this term.

10 An extension of this view of the secularisation process has been attempted by Fenn (1969, 1970).

11 See also Berkes (1964:5) re: Catholicism. 'Secularisation or Laicisation meant the transformation of persons, offices, properties, institutions or matters of an ecclesiastical or spatial character to lay, or worldly, positions.'

12 Berger (1967) extends the usage to include functional transformation and structural transformation.

13 Yinger (1971: chapter 9). For further detail on Marxism see Zeldin (1969). On science see Gilkey (1970). Robertson (1970:39) uses the term 'surrogate religion' to describe these phenomena.

14 See Mumford (1934) for an historical study of technology, and Merton (1968) for the rise of science in the seventeenth century. See also discussion by G. Walters, 'The Secular Premise' in Walters (1968) for an attempt to rescue religion from technological desacralisation.

15 See Novak (1968) for a discussion of this development. For a discussion of Existentialism see Warnock (1970) and for Humanism, Campbell (1971).

16 The following works were consulted: Luckmann (1967); Berger (1967); Berger (1969a and 1969b); Berger and Luckmann (1966).

17 See Berger (1969a), chapter 3. The chapter on Theodicy does contain a questionable typology on a continuum between rationality and irrationality.

18 Durkheim (1915:46). Under normal circumstances, the move to organic solidarity results in religion embracing smaller and smaller areas of social life (page 170). The essential elements remain, exemplified in the bonds of social solidarity.

19 Other examples include Lenski (1961); Parsons (1966); Meland (1966). For other classifications see Barnes and Becker (1952).

20 H. Becker (1950 and 1932) and 'Current Sacred-Secular Theory and its Development' in Becker and Boskoff (1957).

21 For a discussion of the concept, see Bernstein (1971). A critique which is not dissimilar to the one of secularisation expounded here can be found in Tipps (1973).

Chapter 3 The methodological critique

1 This is reflected in a variety of works in the mainstreams of sociology such as Gouldner (1970) and Friedrichs (1970). It is also found in the philosophy of social science; overviews can be found in Brodbeck (1968) and Natanson (1963).

2 The literature on this topic is quite wide-ranging. A start can be made with Bendix and Berger (1959). See also A. Schutz, 'Concept and Theory Formation in the Social Sciences' in Natanson (1963).

3 Macfarlane (1970:10) referring to M. A. Murray, *Witch-cult in Western Europe*, Oxford, 1921.

4 See *Time* Magazine for journalistic accounts, especially: 'That New Black Magic', in *Time*, 27 September 1968; 'Astrology, Fact and Phenomenon', in *Time*, 21 March 1969; and 'The Occult: A Substitute Faith', in *Time*, 19 June 1972.

5 An assumption which is made, for example, by Glock (1967:29).

6 King (1967:175), states in his findings that his factor and cluster analyses cannot test hypotheses or theories. All he can hope to do is compare his data with a theoretical model. 'Since there is no accepted mathematical procedure for making such a comparison, it must be made by the researcher. . . .'

7 These last three factors also fall within the sphere of social psychology, and a full analysis from this perspective would be relevant, though a little out of place. However, the following will give some of the basic references and material: Krech (1962) and Hollander and Hunt (1967).

8 See also McFarland (1967). He argues that the new religions serve at least three functions: '(1) Pressure chambers for the really disadvantaged; (2) media of expression for the common man, and (3) agencies of a quest for a (vocational symbol)' (page 230). He also states that they arose primarily 'to shelter the masses from the impact of a larger and threatening world. . . .'

9 Allen (1971). The general points in the discussion of the 'club' aspect of Japan's new religions were made by Watanabe (1969).

10 See Boulard (1960). This includes his now famous 'Religious Map and Rural France' showing the areas of religious practice.

11 J. Stretelmeier and A. Meyer, *Geography in World Society*, New York, 1963, quoted in Gay (1971).

12 Gaustad (1962:159). See also his (1968) which emphasises number of churches rather than membership.

13 W. Hotchkiss, *Areal Patterns of Religious Institutions in Cincinnati*, University of Chicago, Department of Geography, Research Paper No. 13, 1959, quoted in Gay (1971:11 ff).

14 Glock and Stak, (1965), chapter 11, 'Religion and Radical Politics: a Comparative Study', in which the Netherlands ranked high, the USA low, and Great Britain appeared midway.

15 For discussions of the concept of cult see Howard Becker, who discusses amorphous, loose textured, uncondensed types of social structure in von Wiese (1932:64); David Martin (1965) discusses ideological and structural individualism; Benton Johnson (1963) talks of other-worldly concern with period perfection; and Bryan Wilson (1959) calls them sub-types of gnostic sects. See also Wallis (1974).

Chapter 4   The theoretical critique

1 One need only consider the discussion of roles in Blizzard's study, where 10 ranging from Scholar to Administrator are outlined. S. W. Blizzard, 'Role Conflicts of the Urban Protestant Parish Minister' in Knudten (1967).

2 The use of the word 'religious' to describe the form of social relationship being discussed should not be taken to signify that it has no *content*. The distinction between form and content is analytic only, and the content element becomes clearer later in the discussion.

3 This point is also made by Worsley (1968:21–35).

4 For a different discussion with a similar conclusion see Becker (1950).

5 Simmel (1957:333).

Bibliography

ABERLE, D. (1962), 'A Note on Relative Deprivation Theory as Applied to Millenarian and Other Cult Movements' in S. Thrupp (ed.), *Millenial Dreams in Action: Comparative Studies in Society and History*, Supplement II, Mouton, The Hague.

ALLEN C. (1971), 'The Rush Hour of the Gods', *Listener*, 10 June, vol. 85 (2202).

ALPERT, H. (1939), *Emile Durkheim and His Sociology*, Columbia University Press, New York.

ARMER, M. and SCHNAIBERG, A. (1972), 'Measuring Individual Modernity: a near Myth', *American Sociological Review*, 37, 301–16.

ARON, R. (1964), *The Industrial Society: Three Essays on Ideology and Development*, Praeger, New York.

AYER, A. J. (1968), *The Humanist Outlook*, Pemberton, London.

BARNES, H. E. and BECKER, H. (1952), *Social Thoughts from Lore to Science*, 2nd edn, Harren Press, Washington.

BARNETT, S. A. (1973), 'Biological Myths', *New Society*, 12 April.

BECKER, C. (1932), *The Heavenly City of the Eighteenth Century Philosophers*, Yale University Press, New Haven.

BECKER, H. (1932), 'Processes of Secularisation: an ideal-typical analysis with special reference to personality change as affected by population movement. Pt I and Pt II', *Sociological Review*, 24.

BECKER, H. (1950), *Through Values to Social Interpretation*, Drake University Press, Durham, NC.

BECKER, H. and BOSKOFF, A. (eds) (1957), *Modern Sociological Theory, in Continuity and Change*, Dryden Press, New York.

BELL, D. (1960), *The End of Ideology: On the Exhaustion of Political Ideas in the Fifties*, Free Press, Chicago.

BELLAH, R. N. (1958), 'Religious Aspects of Modernization in Turkey and Japan', *American Journal of Sociology*, 64.

BELLAH, R. N. (1964), 'Religious Evolution', *American Sociological Review*, 29.

BELLAH, R. N. (1967), 'Civil Religion in America', *Daedalus*, 96.

BELLAH, R. N. (1965), *Religion and Progress in Modern Asia*, Free Press, New York.

BENDIX, R. (1966), *Max Weber: an Intellectual Portrait*, Methuen, London.

BENDIX, R. and BERGER, B. (1959), 'Images of Society and Problems of Concept Formation in Sociology' in L. Gross (ed.), *Symposium on Sociological Theory*, Harper & Row, New York.

BERGER, P. (1967), 'Religious Institutions' in N. Smelser (ed.), *Sociology: an Introduction*, Wiley, New York.

BERGER, P. (1969a), *The Social Reality of Religion*, Faber & Faber, London.

BERGER, P. (1969b), *A Rumour of Angels: Modern Society and the Rediscovery of the Supernatural*, Allen Lane, The Penguin Press, London.

BERGER, P. and LUCKMANN, T. (1966), *The Social Construction of Reality, a Treatise in the Sociology of Knowledge*, Doubleday, Garden City, New York.

BERKES, N. (1964), *The Development of Secularism in Turkey*, McGill University Press, Montreal.

BERNSTEIN, B. (1965), 'A Sociolinguistic Approach to Social Learning' in J. Gould (ed.), *Penguin Survey of the Social Sciences*, Penguin, Harmondsworth.

BERNSTEIN, H. (1971), 'Modernisation Theory and the Sociological Study of Development', *Journal of Development Studies*, 7 (2), pp. 141–60.

BIERSTEDT, A. (1959), 'Nominal and Real Definitions in Sociological Theory' in L. Gross (ed.), *Symposium on Sociological Theory*, Harper & Row, New York.

BIRNBAUM, N. and LENZER, G. (eds) (1969), *Sociology and Religion; a Book of Readings*, Prentice Hall, Englewood Cliffs, N.J.

BLACKHAM, H. J. (1966), *Religion in a Modern Society*, Constable, London.

BOSWORTH, W. (1962), *Catholicism and Crisis in Modern France: French Catholic Groups at the Threshold of the Fifth Republic*, Princeton University Press.

BOULARD, F. (1960), *An Introduction to Religious Sociology: Pioneer Work in France*, Darton, Longman & Todd, London.

BRAITHWAITE, R. B. (1953), *Scientific Explanation*, Cambridge University Press.

BRODBECK, M. (ed.) (1968), *Readings in the Philosophy of the Social Sciences*, Macmillan, New York.

BUDD, S. (1973), *Varieties of Unbelief*, quoted in S. Budd, *Sociologists and Religion*, Collier-MacMillan, London.

BUTTERFIELD, H. (1957), *The Origin of Modern Science 1300–1800*, Bell, London.

CAMPBELL, C. (1971), *Towards a Sociology of Irreligion*, Macmillan, London.

CAPORALE, R. and GRUMELLI, A. (eds) (1971), *The Culture of Unbelief*, University of California Press, Berkeley.

CASSIRER, E. (1951), *The Philosophy of the Enlightenment*, Princeton University Press.

CLEBSCH, W. A. (1969), 'American Religion and the Cure of Souls' in D. E. Cutler (ed.), *The World Yearbook of Religion: the Religious Situation*, vol. II, Beacon Press, Boston.

COHEN, M. (1964), 'Baseball as a National Religion' in L. Schneider (ed.), *Religion, Culture and Society*, Wiley, New York.

COHN, W. (1969), 'On the Problem of Religion in Non-Western Cultures', *International Yearbook for the Sociology of Religion*, V, 1969.

COLES, R. W. (1975), 'Football as a "Surrogate" Religion?' in M. Hill (ed.), *A Sociological Yearbook of Religion in Britain*, 8, SCM Press, London.

COMTE, A. (1876), *System of Positive Polity*, vol. III, trans. H. Martineau.

COTGROVE, S. (1967), *The Science of Society: an Introduction to Sociology*, Allen & Unwin, London.

COX, H. (1968), *The Secular City: Secularization and Urbanization in Theological Perspective*, Penguin, Harmondsworth.

CUTLER, D. E. (ed.) (1968, 1969), *The World Yearbook of Religion: The Religious Situation*, vol. I; vol. II; Beacon Press, Boston.

DAMPIER, W. C. (1948), *A History of Science and its Relations with Philosophy and Religion*, Cambridge University Press, 4th edn.

DANSETTE, A. (1961), *Religious History of Modern France*, Herder, Freiburg.

DEMERATH III, N. J. (1965), *Social Class in American Protestantism*, Rand McNally, Chicago.

DEMERATH III, N. J. (1967), 'In a Sow's Ear: A Reply to Goode', *Journal for the Scientific Study of Religion*, VI (1).

DOUGLAS, M. (1966), *Purity and Danger: an Analysis of Concept of Pollution and Taboo*, Routledge & Kegan Paul, London.

DOUGLAS, M. (1970), *Natural Symbols: Explorations in Cosmology*, Barrie & Rockliffe, The Cresset Press, London.

DURKHEIM, E. (1915), *The Elementary Forms of the Religious Life*, trans. by J. W. Swain, Allen & Unwin, London.

DURKHEIM, E. (1933), *The Division of Labour in Society*, trans. G. Simpson, Free Press, Chicago, 5th edn.

DURKHEIM, E. (1938), *The Rules of Sociological Method*, Free Press, Chicago.

DURKHEIM, E. (1947), *Professional Ethics and Civil Morals*, trans. C. Brookfield, Routledge & Kegan Paul, London.

DYNES, R. R. (1955), 'Church-Sect Typology and Socio-Economic Status', *American Sociological Review*, 20 (5).

DYNES, R. R. (1957), 'The Consequences of Sectarianism for Social Participation', *Social Forces*, 35 (4).

ECKHARDT, A. R. (1958), *The Surge of Piety in America: an Appraisal*, Association Press, New York.

EISTER, A. W. (1967), 'Toward a Radical Critique of Church-Sect Typology', *Journal for the Scientific Study of Religion*, VI (1).

FARIS, R. E. (ed.) (1968), *Handbook of Modern Sociology*, Rand McNally, Chicago.

FENN, R. K. (1969), 'The Secularisation of Values', *Journal for the Scientific Study of Religion*, vol. VIII (1).

FENN, R. K. (1970), 'The Process of Secularization: A Post-Parsonian View', *Journal for the Scientific Study of Religion*, vol. IX (2).

FEUER, L. S. (1965), *The Scientific Intellectual: the Psychological and Sociological Origin of Modern Science*, Basic Books, New York.

125

I

FOGARTY, M. P. (1957), *Christian Democracy in Western Europe 1820–1953*, University of Notre Dame Press, South Bend.

FRANKFORT, H. *et al.* (1949), *Before Philosophy. The Intellectual Adventure of Ancient Man*, Penguin, Harmondsworth.

FRIEDRICHS, R. W. (1970), *A Sociology of Sociology*, Free Press, New York.

FROMM, E. (1950), *Psychoanalysis and Religion*, Yale University Press.

GAUSTAD, E. (1962), *Historical Atlas of Religion in America*, Harper & Row, New York.

GAUSTAD, E. (1968), 'America's Institutions on Faith' in D. E. Cutler (ed.), *The World Yearbook of Religion: the Religious Situation*, vol. I, Beacon Press, Boston.

GAY, J. (1971), *The Geography of Religion in England*, Duckworth, London.

GELLNER, E. (1974), 'French Eighteenth Century Materialism' in D. J. O'Connor (ed.), *A Critical History of Western Philosophy*, Free Press, London.

GERTH, H. H. and MILLS, C. W. (eds) (1968), *From Max Weber: Essays in Sociology*, Routledge & Kegan Paul, London.

GIDDENS, A. (1972), 'Four Myths in the History of Social Thought', *Economy and Society*, 1 (4), 351–85.

GILKEY, L. (1970), 'Religious Dimensions of Scientific Enquiry', *Journal of Religion*, 50.

GLASNER, A. M. (1970), 'An Analysis of the Relationship between Different Organisational Situations and the Structure and Latent Conflicts of the Role of the Cleric: A Critical Review of the Literature', unpublished MSc thesis, University of London.

GLASNER, P. E. (1975), ' "Idealisation" and the Social Myth of Secularisation' in M. Hill (ed.), *A Sociological Yearbook of Religion in Britain*, 8, SCM Press, London.

GLOCK, C. Y. (1967), 'Comment on "Pluralism, Religion, and Secularism" ', *Journal for the Scientific Society of Religion*, vol. VI (1).

GLOCK, C. Y. (1971), 'The Study of Unbelief: Perspectives and Research' in R. Caporale and A. Grumelli (eds), *The Culture of Unbelief*, University of California Press, Berkeley.

GLOCK, C. Y. and STARK, R. (1965), *Religion and Society in Tension*, Rand McNally, Chicago.

GOLDMAN, R. (1964), *Religious Thinking from Childhood to Adolescence*, Routledge & Kegan Paul, London.

GOLDSCHMIDT, D. (1962), 'Die religionssoziologische Forschung in der Bundesrepublik Deutschland', *Kölner Zeitschrift für Soziologie und Sozialpsychologie*, vol. 6.

GOODE, E. (1967), 'Some Critical Observations on the Church-Sect Dimension', *Journal for the Scientific Study of Religion*, VI (1).

GOODE, E. (1968), 'Class Styles of Religious Sociation', *British Journal of Sociology*, XIX (1).

GOULD, J. (ed.) (1965), *Penguin Survey of the Social Sciences*, Penguin, Harmondsworth.

GOULDNER, A. (1970), *The Coming Crisis in Western Sociology*, Heinemann, London.

126

GREELEY, A. M. (1970), 'Superstition, Ecstasy and Tribal Consciousness', *Social Research*, 37 (2).

GROETHUYSEN, B. (1934), 'Secularism' in E. R. A. Seligman and A. Johnson (eds), *Encyclopaedia of the Social Sciences*, Macmillan, New York, vol. XIII, p. 631.

GURVITCH, G. (ed.) (1960), *Traité de Sociologie*, vol. V, Presses Universitaires de France, Paris.

GUSTAFSON, P. M. (1967), 'UO–US–PS–PO: A Restatement of Troeltsch's Church-Sect Typology', *Journal for the Scientific Study of Religion*, VI (1).

GUSTAFSSON, B. (1965), 'The State of Sociology of Protestantism in Scandinavia', *Social Compass*, XII.

HALSEY, A. (ed.) (1972), *Trends in British Society since 1960: a Guide to the Changing Social Structure of Britain*, Macmillan, London.

HAMMOND, P. (1967), 'Religion and the Informing Culture' in R. D. Knudten (ed.), *The Sociology of Religion: an Anthology*, Appleton-Century-Crofts, New York, chap. 6.

HAZARD, P. (1953), *The European Mind 1680–1715*, Hollis & Carter, London.

HAZARD, P. (1954), *European Thought in the Eighteenth Century: from Montesquieu to Lessing*, trans. J. L. May, Hollis & Carter, London.

HEMPEL, C. (1952), *Fundamentals of Concept Formation in Empirical Science*, University of Chicago Press, International Encyclopaedia of Unified Science, vol. II, no. 7.

HERBERG, W. (1955), *Protestant–Catholic–Jew: an Essay in American Religious Sociology*, Doubleday, New York.

HERBERG, W. (1967a), 'Religion in Secularized Society: The New Shape of Religion in America' in R. D. Knudten (ed.), *The Sociology of Religion: an Anthology*, Appleton-Century-Crofts, New York, chap. 43.

HERBERG, W. (1967b), 'Religion in Secularized Society: Some Aspects of America's Three-Religion Pluralism' in R. D. Knudten (ed.), *The Sociology of Religion: an Anthology*, Appleton-Century-Crofts, New York, chap. 47.

HIGHET, J. (1950), *The Churches of Scotland Today: a Survey of their Principles, Strength, Work and Statements*, Jackson, Glasgow.

HIGHET, J. (1960), *The Scottish Churches: a Review of their Shape 400 Years after the Reformation*, Skeffington & Sons, London.

HILL, CHRISTOPHER (1965), *The Intellectual Origin of the English Revolution*, Oxford University Press.

HILL, M. (1973), *A Sociology of Religion*, Heinemann, London.

HILL, M. (ed.) (1971), *A Sociological Yearbook of Religion in Britain*, vol. 4, SCM Press, London.

HINDESS, B. (1973), *The Use of Official Statistics in Sociology*, Macmillan, London.

HOLLANDER, E. and HUNT, R. (eds) (1967), *Current Perspectives in Social Psychology*, Oxford University Press.

HOLYOAKE, G. J. (1896), *The Origin and Nature of Secularism*, London.

127

ICHIRO, H. (1968), *Folk Religion in Japan: Continuity and Change*, University of Chicago Press.

IKADO, F. (1968), 'Trends and Problems of New Religions: Religion in Urban Society', *Journal of Asian and African Studies*, vol. III.

ISHWARAN, K. (ed.) (1968), 'Japanese Religion – Special Issue January–April 1968', *Journal of Asian and African Studies*, vol. III, nos 1 and 2.

JACKSON, J. and JOBLING, R. (1968), 'Towards an Analysis of Contemporary Cults' in D. A. Martin (ed.), *A Sociological Yearbook of Religion in Britain*, vol. I, SCM Press, London.

JOHNSON, B. (1963), 'On Church and Sect', *American Sociological Review*, 28.

JOHNSON, H. M. (1961), *Sociology: a Systematic Introduction*, Routledge & Kegan Paul, London.

KING, M. (1967), 'Measuring the Religious Variable: Nine Proposed Dimensions', *Journal for the Scientific Study of Religion*, vol. VI (2).

KNUDTEN, R. (ed.) (1967), *The Sociology of Religion: an Anthology*, Appleton-Century-Crofts, New York.

KOESTLER, A. *et al.* (1950), *The God that Failed: six Studies in Communism*, Hamish Hamilton, London.

KRAUSZ, E. (1972), 'Religion as a Key Variable' in E. Gittus (ed.), *Key Variables in Social Research, Vol. 1*, Heinemann Educational Books for the British Sociological Association, London.

KRECH, D. (ed.) (1962), *Individual in Society*, McGraw-Hill, New York.

LANDIS, B. Y. (ed.) (1961), *Yearbook of American Churches: Information on all Faiths in the U.S.A.*, National Council of the Churches of Christ in the USA, New York.

LE BRAS, G. (1963), 'Déchristianisation: Mot Fallacieux', *Social Compass*, X (6).

LE BRAS, G. *et al.* (1966), 'La vie religieuse' in *Panorama de la France*, La documentation française, Paris.

LENSKI, G. (1961), *The Religious Factor: a Sociological Study of Religion's Impact on Politics, Ceremonies, and Family Life*, Doubleday, Garden City, New York.

LÉVI-STRAUSS, C. (1963), *Structural Anthropology*, Basic Books, New York.

LINTON, R. (1936), *The Study of Man: an Introduction*, Appleton-Century-Crofts, New York.

LIPSET, S. M. (1963), *The First New Nation: the United States in Historical and Comparative Perspective*, Basic Books, New York.

LUCKMANN, T. (1967), *The Invisible Religion: the Problem of Religion and Modern Society*, Macmillan, New York.

LYND, R. S. and LYND H. M. (1929), *Middletown: a Study in American Culture*, Harcourt Brace, New York.

LYND, R. S. and LYND, H. M. (1937), *Middletown in Transition: a Study in Cultural Conflicts*, Harcourt Brace, New York.

MCFARLAND, H. NEILL (1967), *The Rush Hour of the Gods: a Study of New Religious Movements in Japan*, Macmillan, London.

MACFARLANE, A. (1970), *Witchcraft in Tudor and Stuart England: a Regional and Comparative Study*, Routledge & Kegan Paul, London.

MACINTYRE, A. C. (1967), *Secularisation and Moral Change*, Oxford University Press.

MACINTYRE, A. (ed.) (1957), *Metaphysical Beliefs: Three Essays*, SCM Press, London.

MACKENZIE, R. T. and SILVER, A. (1968), *Angels in Marble: Working Class Conservatives in Urban England*. Heinemann, London.

MCKINNEY, J. C. AND TIRYAKIAN, E. A. (eds) (1970), *Theoretical Sociology: Perspectives and Developments*, Appleton-Century-Crofts, New York.

MCLOUGHLIN, N. G. and BELLAII, R. N. (eds) (1968), *Religion in America*, Houghton Mifflin, Boston.

MADGE, C. (1964), *Society and the Mind: Elements of Social Eidos*, Faber & Faber, London.

MARANDA, P. (ed.) (1972), *Mythology*, Penguin, Harmondsworth.

MARSH, ROBERT M. (1967), *Comparative Sociology: a Codification of Cross-societal Analysis*, Harcourt Brace & World, New York.

MARTIN, B. (1968), 'Comments on some Gallup Poll Statistics' in D. A. Martin (ed.), *A Sociological Yearbook of Religion in Britain*, vol. I, SCM Press, London.

MARTIN, DAVID A. (1962), 'The Denomination', *British Journal of Sociology*, 13 (2).

MARTIN, DAVID A. (1965), *Pacifism: an Historical and Sociological Study*, Routledge & Kegan Paul, London.

MARTIN, DAVID A. (1967), *A Sociology of English Religion*, Heinemann, London.

MARTIN, DAVID A. (ed.) (1968, 1969a), *A Sociological Yearbook of Religion in Britain*, vols 1 and 2, SCM Press, London.

MARTIN, DAVID A. (1969b), *The Religious and the Secular, Studies in Secularization*, Routledge & Kegan Paul, London.

MARTIN, D. A. and HILL, M. (eds) (1970), *A Sociological Yearbook of Religion in Britain*, vol. 3, SCM Press, London.

MARTY, M. E. (1959), *The New Shape of American Religion*, Harper & Row, New York.

MARX, K. and ENGELS, F. (1964), *On Religion*, Schocken, New York.

MATTHES, J. (1962), 'Bemerkungen zur Säkularisierungsthese in der neueren Religionssoziologie', *Kölner Zeitschrift für Soziologie und Sozialpsychologie*, vol. 6.

MEHL, R. (1970), *The Sociology of Protestantism*, SCM Press, London.

MELAND, B. (1966), *The Secularisation of Modern Cultures*, Oxford University Press, New York.

MERTON, R. K. (1968), *Social Theory and Social Structure*, Free Press, New York.

MERTON, R. K., BROOM, L. and COTTRELL, L. (eds) (1959), *Sociology Today: Problems and Prospects*, Basic Books, New York.

MOBERG, D. (1962), *The Church as a Social Institution: the Sociology of American Religion*, Prentice-Hall, Englewood Cliffs, New Jersey.

MOL, H. (ed.) (1972), *Western Religion*, Mouton, The Hague.

MORIOKA, K. (1970), 'A Bibliography on the Sociology of Japanese Religions', *Social Compass*, XVII (1).

129

MORIOKA, K. and NEWELL, W. (eds) (1968), *The Sociology of Japanese Religion*, E. J. Brill, Leiden.

MUMFORD, L. (1934), *Technics and Civilization*, Routledge, London.

MURRAY, M. A. (1921), *The Witch-cult in Western Europe: a Study in Anthropology*, Oxford University Press.

MYRDAL, G. (1944), *An American Dilemma: the Negro Problem and Modern Democracy*, Harper, New York.

NATANSON, M. (ed.) (1963), *Philosophy of the Social Sciences: A Reader*, Random House, New York.

NELSON, G. K. (1968), 'The Concept of Cult', *Sociological Review*, 16 (3), new series.

NELSON, G. K. (1969), *Spiritualism and Society*, Routledge & Kegan Paul, London.

NIEBUHR, H. R. (1954), *The Social Sources of Denominationalism*, Shoestring Press, Connecticut.

NIERMANN, E. (1970), Laicism, pt II of 'Secularism' in K. Rahner (ed.), *Sacramentum Mundi: an Encyclopedia of Theology*, vol. VI, Seabury, New York.

NISBET, R. (1970), *The Social Bond: an Introduction to the Study of Society*, Alfred Knopf, New York.

NORBECK, E. (1970), *Religion and Society in Modern Japan: Continuity and Change*, Tourmaline Press, Houston.

NOVAK, M. (1968), 'The New Relativism in American Theology' in D. E. Cutler (ed.), *The World Yearbook of Religion: the Religious Situation*, vol. 1, Beacon Press, Boston.

O'DEA, T. F. (1961), 'Five Dilemmas in the Institutionalization of Religion', *Journal for the Scientific Study of Religion*, vol. 1 (1).

PARK, R. E. (1952), *Human Communities: the City and Human Ecology*, Free Press, Chicago.

PARSONS, T. (1937), *The Structure of Social Action: a Study in Social Theory with Reference to a Group of Recent European Writers*, Free Press, Chicago.

PARSONS, T. (1958), 'The Pattern of Religious Organization in the United States', *Daedalus*, vol. 87.

PARSONS, T. (1960), *Structure and Process in Modern Societies*, Free Press, Chicago.

PARSONS, T. (1966), *Societies: Evolutionary and Comparative Perspectives*, Prentice-Hall, Englewood Cliffs, New Jersey.

PARSONS, T. (1967), *Sociological Theory and Modern Society*, Free Press, New York.

PARSONS, T. *et al.* (eds) (1961), *Theories of Society: Foundation of Modern Sociological Theory*, Free Press, New York.

PETERSEN, W. (1962), 'Religious Statistics in the United States', *Journal for the Scientific Study of Religion*, 1 (2).

PFAUTZ, H. W. (1955), 'Sociology of Secularisation: religious groups', *American Journal of Sociology*, 61.

PFAUTZ, H. W. (1956), 'Christian Science: A Case Study of the Social Psychological Aspect of Secularization', *Social Forces*, 34 (2).

PIAGET, J. and INHELDER, B. (1958), *The Growth of Logical Thinking from Childhood to Adolescence: an Essay on the Construction of Formal Operational Structures*, trans. A. Parsons and S. Milgram, Basic Books, New York.

PICKERING, W. (1968), 'Religion – a Leisure-time Pursuit?' in D. A. Martin (ed.), *A Sociological Yearbook of Religion in Britain*, vol. I, SCM Press, London.

REDFIELD, R. (1947), 'The Folk Society', *American Journal of Sociology*, LII.

REDFIELD, R. (1953), *The Primitive World and its Transformation*, Cornell University Press, Ithaca, New York.

RIEFF, P. (1959), *Freud: the Mind of the Moralist*, Viking Press, New York.

RIEFF, P. (1966), *The Triumph of the Therapeutic: Uses of Faith after Freud*, Harper & Row, New York.

ROBERTSON, R. (1970), *The Sociological Interpretation of Religion*, Basil Blackwell, Oxford.

ROUCEK, J. S. (ed.) (1959), *Contemporary Sociology*, Peter Owen, London.

RUSTIN, M. J. (1971), 'Structural and Unconscious Implications of the Dyad and Triad: an Essay in Theoretical Integration; Durkheim, Simmel, Freud', *Sociological Review*, vol. 19 (2), new series.

SCHARF, B. R. (1970), *The Sociological Study of Religion*, Hutchinson, London.

SCHNEIDER, L. (1970), *A Sociological Approach to Religion*, Wiley, New York.

SCHNEIDER, L. (ed.) (1964), *Religion, Culture and Society: a Reader in the Sociology of Religion*, Wiley, New York.

SCHUTZ, A. (1962), *Collected Papers Vol. I: The Problem of Social Reality*, Martinus Nijhoff, The Hague.

SCHUTZ, A. (1963), 'Concept and Theory Formation in the Social Sciences' in M. Natanson (ed.), *Philosophy of the Social Sciences: A Reader*, Random House, New York.

SCOTFORD-ARCHER, M. and VAUGHAN, M. (1970), 'Education, Secularization, Desecularization and Resecularization' in D. A. Martin and M. Hill (eds), *A Sociological Yearbook of Religion in Britain*, vol. 3, SCM Press, London.

SELIGMAN, E. R. A. and JOHNSON, A. (eds) (1934), *Encyclopaedia of the Social Sciences*, Macmillan, New York.

SHILS, E. and YOUNG, M. (1953), 'The Meaning of the Coronation', *Sociological Review*, I (2), new series.

SHINER, L. (1967), 'The Concept of Secularization in Empirical Research', *Journal for the Scientific Study of Religion*, vol. VI.

SIMMEL, G. (1950), 'Metropolis and Mental Life' in G. Wolff (ed.), *The Sociology of Georg Simmel*, Free Press, Chicago.

SIMMEL, G. (1957), 'A Contribution to the Sociology of Religion', *American Journal of Sociology*, II, 1905, reprinted in J. M. Yinger, *Religion, Society and the Individual*, Macmillan, New York.

SIMMEL, G. (1959), *The Sociology of Religion*, trans. C. Rosenthal, The Philosophical Library, New York.

131

SJOBERG, G. (1952), 'Folk and "Feudal" Societies', *American Journal of Sociology*, LVIII.

SKLAIR L. (1970), *The Sociology of Progress*, Routledge & Kegan Paul, London.

SMITH, D. E. (1963), *India as a Secular State*, Princeton University Press.

SMITH, W. ROBERTSON (1894), *Lectures on the Religion of the Semites*, A. & C. Black, London.

SOROKIN, P. (1966), 'The Western Religion and Morality of Today', *International Yearbook for the Sociology of Religion*, II.

SPIRO, M. E. (1969), 'Religion: Problems of Definition and Explanation' in M. Banton (ed.), *Anthropological Approaches to the Study of Religion*, Tavistock Publications, London (2nd imp.).

STARK, R. and GLOCK, C. Y. (1968), *American Piety: the Nature of Religious Commitment*, University of California Press, Berkeley.

STARK, W. (1967), *The Sociology of Religion: a Study of Christendom*, Routledge & Kegan Paul, London.

STROUP, H. H. (1945), *The Jehovah's Witnesses*, Russell & Russell, New York.

SUMNER, W. G. (1906), *Folkways: a Study of the Sociological Importance of Usages, Manners, Customs, Mores and Morals*, Ginn, Boston.

SWANSON, G. (1968), 'Modern Secularity' in D. E. Cutler (ed.), *World Yearbook of Religion: the Religious Situation*, vol. I, Beacon Press, Boston.

THOMAS, K. V. (1971), *Religion and the Decline of Magic: Studies in Popular Beliefs in Sixteenth and Seventeenth Century England*, Weidenfeld & Nicolson, London.

THOMSEN, HARRY (1963), *The New Religions of Japan*, Tuttle, Rutland, Vermont.

TIME (1968), 'That New Black Magic', *Time*, 27 September.

TIME (1969), 'Astrology, Fact and Phenomenon', *Time*, 21 March.

TIME (1972), 'The Occult: A Substitute Faith', *Time*, 19 June.

TIPPS, D. C. (1973), 'Modernization Theory and the Comparative Study of Society: a Critical Perspective', *Comparative Studies in Society and History*, 15.

TIRYAKIAN, E. A. (ed.) (1963), *Sociological Theory, Values and Socio-Cultural Change: Essays in Honor of Pitirim A. Sorokin*, Free Press, New York.

TÖNNIES, F. (1955), *Community and Association*, trans. C. P. Loomis, Routledge & Kegan Paul, London.

TOULMIN, S. (1957), 'Contemporary Scientific Mythology' in A. MacIntyre (ed.), *Metaphysical Beliefs*, SCM Press, London.

TOWLER, R. (1974), *Homo Religiosus: Sociological Problems in the Study of Religion*, Constable, London.

TROELTSCH, E. (1931), *The Social Teachings of the Christian Churches*, Macmillan, New York.

TROELTSCH, E. (1955), *Protestantism and Progress: a Historical Study of the Relation of Protestantism to the Modern World*, Putman's, London.

TRUZZI, M. (1972), 'The Occult Revival as Pop Culture: Some Random

Observations on the Old and Noueau Witch', *Sociological Quarterly*, 13 (1).

TUCKER, R. C. (1961), *Philosophy and Myth in Karl Marx*, Cambridge University Press.

VAHANIAN, G. (1961), *The Death of God: the Culture of our Post-Christian Era*, George Brazillier, New York.

VERBIT, M. F. (1970), 'The Components and Dimensions of Religious Behaviour: Toward a Reconceptualization of Religiosity' in P. E. Hammond and B. Johnson (eds), *American Mosaic*, Random House, New York.

VERNON, G. M. (1962), *Sociology and Religion*, McGraw Hill, New York.

VOGT, E. (1966), 'The Sociology of Protestantism in Norway', *Social Compass*, XIII.

WALLIS, R. (1974), 'Ideology, Authority and the Development of Cultic Movements', *Social Research*, 41 (2).

WALLIS, R. (1975), 'Relative Deprivation and Social Movements: a cautionary note', *British Journal of Sociology*, XXVI, 3.

WALTERS, G. (ed.) (1968), *Religion in a Technological Society*, Bath University Press.

WARNER, W. LLOYD (1962), *American Life: Dream and Reality*, University of Chicago Press.

WARNOCK, MARY (1970), *Existentialism*, Oxford University Press.

WATANABE, E. (1969), 'A Sociological Observation of *Rissho Kosei Kai*', unpublished paper, Graduate Seminar in the Sociology of Religion, London School of Economics, 27 November.

WEBER, MAX (1930), *The Protestant Ethic and the Spirit of Capitalism*, trans. T. Parsons, Free Press, Chicago.

WEBER, MAX (1947), *The Theory of Social and Economic Organization*, trans. A. R. Henderson and T. Parsons, Free Press, Chicago.

WEBER, MAX (1958), *The Religions of India: the Sociology of Hinduism and Buddhism*, trans. H. H. Gerth and D. Martindale, Free Press, Chicago.

WEBER, MAX (1963), *The Sociology of Religion*, trans. by E. Fischoff, Beacon Press, Boston.

WEBER, MAX (1964), *The Theory of Social and Economic Organisation*, T. Parsons (ed.), Free Press, New York.

WEBER, MAX (1968), *Economy and Society: an Outline of Interpretive Sociology*, ed. G. Roth and G. Wittich, Bedminster Press, Totowa, New Jersey.

WEIGERT, A. J. and THOMAS, D. L. (1970), 'Socialization and Religiosity: A Cross-National Analysis of Catholic Adolescents', *Sociometry*, vol. 33 (3).

WIESE, LEOPOLD M. W. VON (1932), *Systematic Sociology*, adapted and amplified by H. Becker, Wiley, New York.

WILLER, D. and WILLER, J. (1973), *Systematic Empiricism: a Critique of a Pseudo-science*, Prentice-Hall, Englewood Cliffs.

WILSON, B. R. (1959), 'An Analysis of Sect Development', *American Sociological Review*, 24 (1).

133

WILSON, B. R. (1966), *Religion in Secular Society: a Sociological Comment*, Watts, London.

WILSON, B. R. (ed.) (1967), *Patterns of Sectarianism: Organisation and Ideology in Social and Religious Movements*, Heinemann, London.

WILSON, B. R. (1968), 'Religion and the Churches in Contemporary America' in W. G. McLoughlin and R. N. Bellah (eds), *Religion in America*, Beacon Press, Boston.

WILSON, B. R. (1970), *Religious Sects: a Sociological Study*, Weidenfeld & Nicolson, London.

WOLFF, K. (ed.) (1950), *The Sociology of Georg Simmel*, Free Press, Chicago.

WORSLEY, P. M. (1968), *The Trumpet Shall Sound: a Study of 'Cargo' Cults in Melanesia*, Paladin, London.

YANG, C. K. (1970), *Religion in Chinese Society*, University of California Press, Berkeley.

YINGER, J. M. (1957), *Religion, Society, and the Individual: an Introduction to the Sociology of Religion*, Macmillan, New York.

YINGER, J. M. (1971), *The Scientific Study of Religion*, Macmillan, New York.

ZELDIN, M. B. (1969), 'The Religious Nature of Russian Marxism', *Journal for the Scientific Study of Religion*, vol. VIII, no. 1.

ZETTERBERG, H. (1954), *On Theory and Verification in Sociology*, Bedminster Press, Totowa, New Jersey.

Index

Routledge Social Science Series

Routledge & Kegan Paul   London, Henley and Boston

39 Store Street, London WC1E 7DD
Broadway House, Newtown Road, Henley-on-Thames,
Oxon RG9 1EN
9 Park Street, Boston, Mass. 02108

Contents

*Authors wishing to submit manuscripts for any series in
this catalogue should send them to the Social Science Editor,
Routledge & Kegan Paul Ltd, 39 Store Street,
London WC1E 7DD*

●*Books so marked are available in paperback*
All books are in Metric Demy 8vo format (216 × 138mm approx.)

International Library of Sociology

General Editor   John Rex

GENERAL SOCIOLOGY

Barnsley, J. H. The Social Reality of Ethics. *464 pp.*
Belshaw, Cyril. The Conditions of Social Performance. *An Exploratory Theory. 144 pp.*
Brown, Robert. Explanation in Social Science. *208 pp.*
●   Rules and Laws in Sociology. *192 pp.*
Bruford, W. H. Chekhov and His Russia. *A Sociological Study. 244 pp.*
Cain, Maureen E. Society and the Policeman's Role. *326 pp.*
●**Fletcher, Colin.** Beneath the Surface. *An Account of Three Styles of Sociological Research. 221 pp.*
Gibson, Quentin. The Logic of Social Enquiry. *240 pp.*
Glucksmann, M. Structuralist Analysis in Contemporary Social Thought. *212 pp.*
Gurvitch, Georges. Sociology of Law. *Preface by Roscoe Pound. 264 pp.*
Hodge, H. A. Wilhelm Dilthey. *An Introduction. 184 pp.*
Homans, George C. Sentiments and Activities. *336 pp.*
Johnson, Harry M. Sociology: *a Systematic Introduction. Foreword by Robert K. Merton. 710 pp.*
●**Keat, Russell,** and **Urry, John.** Social Theory as Science. *278 pp.*
Mannheim, Karl. Essays on Sociology and Social Psychology. *Edited by Paul Keckskemeti. With Editorial Note by Adolph Lowe. 344 pp.*
Systematic Sociology: *An Introduction to the Study of Society. Edited by J. S. Erös and Professor W. A. C. Stewart. 220 pp.*
Martindale, Don. The Nature and Types of Sociological Theory. *292 pp.*
●**Maus, Heinz.** A Short History of Sociology. *234 pp.*
Mey, Harald. Field-Theory. *A Study of its Application in the Social Sciences. 352 pp.*
Myrdal, Gunnar. Value in Social Theory: *A Collection of Essays on Methodology. Edited by Paul Streeten. 332 pp.*
Ogburn, William F., and **Nimkoff, Meyer F.** A Handbook of Sociology. *Preface by Karl Mannheim. 656 pp. 46 figures. 35 tables.*
Parsons, Talcott, and **Smelser, Neil J.** Economy and Society: *A Study in the Integration of Economic and Social Theory. 362 pp.*
Podgórecki, Adam. Practical Social Sciences. *About 200 pp.*
●**Rex, John.** Key Problems of Sociological Theory. *220 pp.*
Sociology and the Demystification of the Modern World. *282 pp.*
●**Rex, John** (Ed.) Approaches to Sociology. *Contributions by Peter Abell, Frank Bechhofer, Basil Bernstein, Ronald Fletcher, David Frisby, Miriam Glucksmann, Peter Lassman, Herminio Martins, John Rex, Roland Robertson, John Westergaard and Jock Young. 302 pp.*
Rigby, A. Alternative Realities. *352 pp.*
Roche, M. Phenomenology, Language and the Social Sciences. *374 pp.*

3

Sahay, A. Sociological Analysis. *220 pp.*
Simirenko, Alex (Ed.) Soviet Sociology. *Historical Antecedents and Current Appraisals. Introduction by Alex Simirenko. 376 pp.*
Strasser, Hermann. The Normative Structure of Sociology. *Conservative and Emancipatory Themes in Social Thought. About 340 pp.*
Urry, John. Reference Groups and the Theory of Revolution. *244 pp.*
Weinberg, E. Development of Sociology in the Soviet Union. *173 pp.*

FOREIGN CLASSICS OF SOCIOLOGY

●Durkheim, Emile. Suicide. *A Study in Sociology. Edited and with an Introduction by George Simpson. 404 pp.*
●Gerth, H. H., and Mills, C. Wright. From Max Weber: *Essays in Sociology. 502 pp.*
●Tönnies, Ferdinand. Community and Association. (*Gemeinschaft und Gesellschaft.*) *Translated and Supplemented by Charles P. Loomis. Foreword by Pitirim A. Sorokin. 334 pp.*

SOCIAL STRUCTURE

Andreski, Stanislav. Military Organization and Society. *Foreword by Professor A. R. Radcliffe-Brown. 226 pp. 1 folder.*
Carlton, Eric. Ideology and Social Order. *Preface by Professor Philip Abrahams. About 320 pp.*
Coontz, Sydney H. Population Theories and the Economic Interpretation. *202 pp.*
Coser, Lewis. The Functions of Social Conflict. *204 pp.*
Dickie-Clark, H. F. Marginal Situation: *A Sociological Study of a Coloured Group. 240 pp. 11 tables.*
Glaser, Barney, and Strauss, Anselm L. Status Passage. *A Formal Theory. 208 pp.*
Glass, D. V. (Ed.) Social Mobility in Britain. *Contributions by J. Berent, T. Bottomore, R. C. Chambers, J. Floud, D. V. Glass, J. R. Hall, H. T. Himmelweit, R. K. Kelsall, F. M. Martin, C. A. Moser, R. Mukherjee, and W. Ziegel. 420 pp.*
Johnstone, Frederick A. Class, Race and Gold. *A Study of Class Relations and Racial Discrimination in South Africa. 312 pp.*
Jones, Garth N. Planned Organizational Change: *An Exploratory Study Using an Empirical Approach. 268 pp.*
Kelsall, R. K. Higher Civil Servants in Britain: *From 1870 to the Present Day. 268 pp. 31 tables.*
König, René. The Community. *232 pp. Illustrated.*
●Lawton, Denis. Social Class, Language and Education. *192 pp.*
McLeish, John. The Theory of Social Change: *Four Views Considered. 128 pp.*
Marsh, David C. The Changing Social Structure of England and Wales, 1871-1961. *288 pp.*
Menzies, Ken. Talcott Parsons and the Social Image of Man. *About 208 pp.*

●**Mouzelis, Nicos.** Organization and Bureaucracy. *An Analysis of Modern Theories. 240 pp.*

Mulkay, M. J. Functionalism, Exchange and Theoretical Strategy. *272 pp.*

Ossowski, Stanislaw. Class Structure in the Social Consciousness. *210 pp.*

●**Podgórecki, Adam.** Law and Society. *302 pp.*

Renner, Karl. Institutions of Private Law and Their Social Functions. *Edited, with an Introduction and Notes, by O. Kahn-Freud. Translated by Agnes Schwarzschild. 316 pp.*

SOCIOLOGY AND POLITICS

Acton, T. A. Gypsy Politics and Social Change. *316 pp.*

Clegg, Stuart. Power, Rule and Domination. *A Critical and Empirical Understanding of Power in Sociological Theory and Organisational Life. About 300 pp.*

Hechter, Michael. Internal Colonialism. *The Celtic Fringe in British National Development, 1536–1966. 361 pp.*

Hertz, Frederick. Nationality in History and Politics: *A Psychology and Sociology of National Sentiment and Nationalism. 432 pp.*

Kornhauser, William. The Politics of Mass Society. *272 pp. 20 tables.*

●**Kroes, R.** Soldiers and Students. *A Study of Right- and Left-wing Students. 174 pp.*

Laidler, Harry W. History of Socialism. *Social-Economic Movements: An Historical and Comparative Survey of Socialism, Communism, Co-operation, Utopianism; and other Systems of Reform and Reconstruction. 992 pp.*

Lasswell, H. D. Analysis of Political Behaviour. *324 pp.*

Martin, David A. Pacifism: *an Historical and Sociological Study. 262 pp.*

Martin, Roderick. Sociology of Power. *About 272 pp.*

Myrdal, Gunnar. The Political Element in the Development of Economic Theory. *Translated from the German by Paul Streeten. 282 pp.*

Wilson, H. T. The American Ideology. *Science, Technology and Organization of Modes of Rationality. About 280 pp.*

Wootton, Graham. Workers, Unions and the State. *188 pp.*

CRIMINOLOGY

Ancel, Marc. Social Defence: *A Modern Approach to Criminal Problems. Foreword by Leon Radzinowicz. 240 pp.*

Cain, Maureen E. Society and the Policeman's Role. *326 pp.*

Cloward, Richard A., and **Ohlin, Lloyd E.** Delinquency and Opportunity: *A Theory of Delinquent Gangs. 248 pp.*

Downes, David M. The Delinquent Solution. *A Study in Subcultural Theory. 296 pp.*

Dunlop, A. B., and **McCabe, S.** Young Men in Detention Centres. *192 pp.*

Friedlander, Kate. The Psycho-Analytical Approach to Juvenile Delinquency: *Theory, Case Studies, Treatment. 320 pp.*

Glueck, Sheldon, and **Eleanor.** Family Environment and Delinquency. *With the statistical assistance of Rose W. Kneznek. 340 pp.*

Lopez-Rey, Manuel. Crime. *An Analytical Appraisal. 288 pp.*

Mannheim, Hermann. Comparative Criminology: *a Text Book. Two volumes. 442 pp. and 380 pp.*

Morris, Terence. The Criminal Area: *A Study in Social Ecology. Foreword by Hermann Mannheim. 232 pp. 25 tables. 4 maps.*

Rock, Paul. Making People Pay. *338 pp.*

● **Taylor, Ian, Walton, Paul,** and **Young, Jock.** The New Criminology. *For a Social Theory of Deviance. 325 pp.*

● **Taylor, Ian, Walton, Paul,** and **Young, Jock** (Eds). Critical Criminology. *268 pp.*

SOCIAL PSYCHOLOGY

Bagley, Christopher. The Social Psychology of the Epileptic Child. *320 pp.*

Barbu, Zevedei. Problems of Historical Psychology. *248 pp.*

Blackburn, Julian. Psychology and the Social Pattern. *184 pp.*

● **Brittan, Arthur.** Meanings and Situations. *224 pp.*

Carroll, J. Break-Out from the Crystal Palace. *200 pp.*

● **Fleming, C. M.** Adolescence: Its Social Psychology. *With an Introduction to recent findings from the fields of Anthropology, Physiology, Medicine, Psychometrics and Sociometry. 288 pp.*

● The Social Psychology of Education: *An Introduction and Guide to Its Study. 136 pp.*

● **Homans, George C.** The Human Group. *Foreword by Bernard DeVoto. Introduction by Robert K. Merton. 526 pp.*

● Social Behaviour: *its Elementary Forms. 416 pp.*

● **Klein, Josephine.** The Study of Groups. *226 pp. 31 figures. 5 tables.*

Linton, Ralph. The Cultural Background of Personality. *132 pp.*

● **Mayo, Elton.** The Social Problems of an Industrial Civilization. *With an appendix on the Political Problem. 180 pp.*

Ottaway, A. K. C. Learning Through Group Experience. *176 pp.*

Plummer, Ken. Sexual Stigma. *An Interactionist Account. 254 pp.*

● **Rose, Arnold M.** (Ed.) Human Behaviour and Social Processes: *an Interactionist Approach. Contributions by Arnold M. Rose, Ralph H. Turner, Anselm Strauss, Everett C. Hughes, E. Franklin Frazier, Howard S. Becker, et al. 696 pp.*

Smelser, Neil J. Theory of Collective Behaviour. *448 pp.*

Stephenson, Geoffrey M. The Development of Conscience. *128 pp.*

Young, Kimball. Handbook of Social Psychology. *658 pp. 16 figures. 10 tables.*

SOCIOLOGY OF THE FAMILY

Banks, J. A. Prosperity and Parenthood: *A Study of Family Planning among The Victorian Middle Classes. 262 pp.*

Bell, Colin R. Middle Class Families: *Social and Geographical Mobility. 224 pp.*

Burton, Lindy. Vulnerable Children. *272 pp.*
Gavron, Hannah. The Captive Wife: *Conflicts of Household Mothers.* *190 pp.*
George, Victor, and **Wilding, Paul.** Motherless Families. *248 pp.*
Klein, Josephine. Samples from English Cultures.
    1. Three Preliminary Studies and Aspects of Adult Life in England. *447 pp.*
    2. Child-Rearing Practices and Index. *247 pp.*
Klein, Viola. The Feminine Character. *History of an Ideology. 244 pp.*
McWhinnie, Alexina M. Adopted Children. *How They Grow Up. 304 pp.*
● **Morgan, D. H. J.** Social Theory and the Family. *About 320 pp.*
● **Myrdal, Alva,** and **Klein, Viola.** Women's Two Roles: *Home and Work.* *238 pp. 27 tables.*
Parsons, Talcott, and **Bales, Robert F.** Family: Socialization and Inter-action Process. *In collaboration with James Olds, Morris Zelditch and Philip E. Slater. 456 pp. 50 figures and tables.*

SOCIAL SERVICES

Bastide, Roger. The Sociology of Mental Disorder. *Translated from the French by Jean McNeil. 260 pp.*
Carlebach, Julius. Caring For Children in Trouble. *266 pp.*
George, Victor. Foster Care. *Theory and Practice. 234 pp.*
    Social Security: *Beveridge and After. 258 pp.*
George, V., and **Wilding, P.** Motherless Families. *248 pp.*
●**Goetschius, George W.** Working with Community Groups. *256 pp.*
Goetschius, George W., and **Tash, Joan.** Working with Unattached Youth. *416 pp.*
Hall, M. P., and **Howes, I. V.** The Church in Social Work. *A Study of Moral Welfare Work undertaken by the Church of England. 320 pp.*
Heywood, Jean S. Children in Care: *the Development of the Service for the Deprived Child. 264 pp.*
Hoenig, J., and **Hamilton, Marian W.** The De-Segregation of the Mentally Ill. *284 pp.*
Jones, Kathleen. Mental Health and Social Policy, 1845-1959. *264 pp.*
King, Roy D., Raynes, Norma V., and **Tizard, Jack.** Patterns of Residential Care. *356 pp.*
Leigh, John. Young People and Leisure. *256 pp.*
●**Mays, John.** (Ed.) Penelope Hall's Social Services of England and Wales. *About 324 pp.*
Morris, Mary. Voluntary Work and the Welfare State. *300 pp.*
Nokes, P. L. The Professional Task in Welfare Practice. *152 pp.*
Timms, Noel. Psychiatric Social Work in Great Britain (1939-1962). *280 pp.*
●   Social Casework: *Principles and Practice. 256 pp.*
Young, A. F. Social Services in British Industry. *272 pp.*

SOCIOLOGY OF EDUCATION

Banks, Olive. Parity and Prestige in English Secondary Education: a Study in Educational Sociology. *272 pp.*

Bentwich, Joseph. Education in Israel. *224 pp. 8 pp. plates.*

●**Blyth, W. A. L.** English Primary Education. *A Sociological Description.*
1. Schools. *232 pp.*
2. Background. *168 pp.*

Collier, K. G. The Social Purposes of Education: *Personal and Social Values in Education. 268 pp.*

Dale, R. R., and **Griffith, S.** Down Stream: *Failure in the Grammar School. 108 pp.*

Evans, K. M. Sociometry and Education. *158 pp.*

●**Ford, Julienne.** Social Class and the Comprehensive School. *192 pp.*

Foster, P. J. Education and Social Change in Ghana. *336 pp. 3 maps.*

Fraser, W. R. Education and Society in Modern France. *150 pp.*

Grace, Gerald R. Role Conflict and the Teacher. *150 pp.*

Hans, Nicholas. New Trends in Education in the Eighteenth Century. *278 pp. 19 tables.*

● Comparative Education: *A Study of Educational Factors and Traditions. 360 pp.*

●**Hargreaves, David.** Interpersonal Relations and Education. *432 pp.*

● Social Relations in a Secondary School. *240 pp.*

Holmes, Brian. Problems in Education. *A Comparative Approach. 336 pp.*

King, Ronald. Values and Involvement in a Grammar School. *164 pp.*
School Organization and Pupil Involvement. *A Study of Secondary Schools.*

●**Mannheim, Karl,** and **Stewart, W. A. C.** An Introduction to the Sociology of Education. *206 pp.*

Morris, Raymond N. The Sixth Form and College Entrance. *231 pp.*

●**Musgrove, F.** Youth and the Social Order. *176 pp.*

●**Ottaway, A. K. C.** Education and Society: An Introduction to the Sociology of Education. *With an Introduction by W. O. Lester Smith. 212 pp.*

Peers, Robert. Adult Education: *A Comparative Study. 398 pp.*

Pritchard, D. G. Education and the Handicapped: *1760 to 1960. 258 pp.*

Stratta, Erica. The Education of Borstal Boys. *A Study of their Educational Experiences prior to, and during, Borstal Training. 256 pp.*

Taylor, P. H., Reid, W. A., and **Holley, B. J.** The English Sixth Form. *A Case Study in Curriculum Research. 200 pp.*

SOCIOLOGY OF CULTURE

Eppel, E. M., and **M.** Adolescents and Morality: *A Study of some Moral Values and Dilemmas of Working Adolescents in the Context of a changing Climate of Opinion. Foreword by W. J. H. Sprott. 268 pp. 39 tables.*

●**Fromm, Erich.** The Fear of Freedom. *286 pp.*

● The Sane Society. *400 pp.*

Mannheim, Karl. Essays on the Sociology of Culture. *Edited by Ernst Mannheim in co-operation with Paul Kecskemeti. Editorial Note by Adolph Lowe. 280 pp.*

Weber, Alfred. Farewell to European History: *or The Conquest of Nihilism. Translated from the German by R. F. C. Hull. 224 pp.*

SOCIOLOGY OF RELIGION

Argyle, Michael and **Beit-Hallahmi, Benjamin.** The Social Psychology of Religion. *About 256 pp.*

Glasner, Peter E. The Sociology of Secularisation. *A Critique of a Concept. About 180 pp.*

Nelson, G. K. Spiritualism and Society. *313 pp.*

Stark, Werner. The Sociology of Religion. *A Study of Christendom.*
    Volume I. *Established Religion. 248 pp.*
    Volume II. *Sectarian Religion. 368 pp.*
    Volume III. *The Universal Church. 464 pp.*
    Volume IV. *Types of Religious Man. 352 pp.*
    Volume V. *Types of Religious Culture. 464 pp.*

Turner, B. S. Weber and Islam. *216 pp.*

Watt, W. Montgomery. Islam and the Integration of Society. *320 pp.*

SOCIOLOGY OF ART AND LITERATURE

Jarvie, Ian C. Towards a Sociology of the Cinema. *A Comparative Essay on the Structure and Functioning of a Major Entertainment Industry. 405 pp.*

Rust, Frances S. Dance in Society. *An Analysis of the Relationships between the Social Dance and Society in England from the Middle Ages to the Present Day. 256 pp. 8 pp. of plates.*

Schücking, L. L. The Sociology of Literary Taste. *112 pp.*

Wolff, Janet. Hermeneutic Philosophy and the Sociology of Art. *150 pp.*

SOCIOLOGY OF KNOWLEDGE

Diesing, P. Patterns of Discovery in the Social Sciences. *262 pp.*

●**Douglas, J. D.** (Ed.) Understanding Everyday Life. *370 pp.*

●**Hamilton, P.** Knowledge and Social Structure. *174 pp.*

Jarvie, I. C. Concepts and Society. *232 pp.*

Mannheim, Karl. Essays on the Sociology of Knowledge. *Edited by Paul Kecskemeti. Editorial Note by Adolph Lowe. 353 pp.*

Remmling, Gunter W. The Sociology cf Karl Mannheim. *With a Bibliographical Guide to the Sociology of Knowledge, Ideological Analysis, and Social Planning. 255 pp.*

Remmling, Gunter W. (Ed.) Towards the Sociology of Knowledge. *Origin and Development of a Sociological Thought Style. 463 pp.*

Stark, Werner. The Sociology of Knowledge: *An Essay in Aid of a Deeper Understanding of the History of Ideas. 384 pp.*

URBAN SOCIOLOGY

Ashworth, William. The Genesis of Modern British Town Planning: *A Study in Economic and Social History of the Nineteenth and Twentieth Centuries. 288 pp.*

Cullingworth, J. B. Housing Needs and Planning Policy: *A Restatement of the Problems of Housing Need and 'Overspill' in England and Wales. 232 pp. 44 tables. 8 maps.*

Dickinson, Robert E. City and Region: *A Geographical Interpretation 608 pp. 125 figures.*

The West European City: *A Geographical Interpretation. 600 pp. 129 maps. 29 plates.*

● The City Region in Western Europe. *320 pp. Maps.*

Humphreys, Alexander J. New Dubliners: *Urbanization and the Irish Family. Foreword by George C. Homans. 304 pp.*

Jackson, Brian. Working Class Community: *Some General Notions raised by a Series of Studies in Northern England. 192 pp.*

Jennings, Hilda. Societies in the Making: *a Study of Development and Re-development within a County Borough. Foreword by D. A. Clark. 286 pp.*

●**Mann, P. H.** An Approach to Urban Sociology. *240 pp.*

Morris, R. N., and **Mogey, J.** The Sociology of Housing. *Studies at Berinsfield. 232 pp. 4 pp. plates.*

Rosser, C., and **Harris, C.** The Family and Social Change. *A Study of Family and Kinship in a South Wales Town. 352 pp. 8 maps.*

●**Stacey, Margaret, Batsone, Eric, Bell, Colin,** and **Thurcott, Anne.** Power, Persistence and Change. *A Second Study of Banbury. 196 pp.*

RURAL SOCIOLOGY

Haswell, M. R. The Economics of Development in Village India. *120 pp.*

Littlejohn, James. Westrigg: *the Sociology of a Cheviot Parish. 172 pp. 5 figures.*

Mayer, Adrian C. Peasants in the Pacific. *A Study of Fiji Indian Rural Society. 248 pp. 20 plates.*

Williams, W. M. The Sociology of an English Village: *Gosforth. 272 pp. 12 figures. 13 tables.*

SOCIOLOGY OF INDUSTRY AND DISTRIBUTION

Anderson, Nels. Work and Leisure. *280 pp.*

●**Blau, Peter M.**, and **Scott, W. Richard.** Formal Organizations: *a Comparative approach. Introduction and Additional Bibliography by J. H. Smith. 326 pp.*

Dunkerley, David. The Foreman. *Aspects of Task and Structure. 192 pp.*

Eldridge, J. E. T. Industrial Disputes. *Essays in the Sociology of Industrial Relations. 288 pp.*

Hetzler, Stanley. Applied Measures for Promoting Technological Growth. *352 pp.*
Technological Growth and Social Change. *Achieving Modernization. 269 pp.*

Hollowell, Peter G. The Lorry Driver. *272 pp.*

●**Oxaal, I., Barnett, T.**, and **Booth, D.** (Eds). Beyond the Sociology of Development. *Economy and Society in Latin America and Africa. 295 pp.*

Smelser, Neil J. Social Change in the Industrial Revolution: *An Application of Theory to the Lancashire Cotton Industry, 1770–1840. 468 pp. 12 figures. 14 tables.*

ANTHROPOLOGY

Ammar, Hamed. Growing up in an Egyptian Village: *Silwa, Province of Aswan. 336 pp.*

Brandel-Syrier, Mia. Reeftown Elite. *A Study of Social Mobility in a Modern African Community on the Reef. 376 pp.*

Dickie-Clark, H. F. The Marginal Situation. *A Sociological Study of a Coloured Group. 236 pp.*

Dube, S. C. Indian Village. *Foreword by Morris Edward Opler. 276 pp. 4 plates.*
India's Changing Villages: *Human Factors in Community Development. 260 pp. 8 plates. 1 map.*

Firth, Raymond. Malay Fishermen. *Their Peasant Economy. 420 pp. 17 pp. plates.*

Gulliver, P. H. Social Control in an African Society: a Study of the Arusha, Agricultural Masai of Northern Tanganyika. *320 pp. 8 plates. 10 figures.*
Family Herds. *288 pp.*

Ishwaran, K. Tradition and Economy in Village India: *An Interactionist Approach.*
Foreword by Conrad Arensburg. 176 pp.

Jarvie, Ian C. The Revolution in Anthropology. *268 pp.*

Little, Kenneth L. Mende of Sierra Leone. *308 pp. and folder.*
Negroes in Britain. *With a New Introduction and Contemporary Study by Leonard Bloom. 320 pp.*

Lowie, Robert H. Social Organization. *494 pp.*

Mayer, A. C. Peasants in the Pacific. *A Study of Fiji Indian Rural Society. 248 pp.*

Meer, Fatima. Race and Suicide in South Africa. *325 pp.*

Smith, Raymond T. The Negro Family in British Guiana: *Family Structure and Social Status in the Villages. With a Foreword by Meyer Fortes. 314 pp. 8 plates. 1 figure. 4 maps.*
Smooha, Sammy. Israel: Pluralism and Conflict. *About 320 pp.*

SOCIOLOGY AND PHILOSOPHY

Barnsley, John H. The Social Reality of Ethics. *A Comparative Analysis of Moral Codes. 448 pp.*
Diesing, Paul. Patterns of Discovery in the Social Sciences. *362 pp.*
●**Douglas, Jack D.** (Ed.) Understanding Everyday Life. *Toward the Reconstruction of Sociological Knowledge. Contributions by Alan F. Blum. Aaron W. Cicourel, Norman K. Denzin, Jack D. Douglas, John Heeren, Peter McHugh, Peter K. Manning, Melvin Power, Matthew Speier, Roy Turner, D. Lawrence Wieder, Thomas P. Wilson and Don H. Zimmerman. 370 pp.*
Gorman, Robert A. The Dual Vision. *Alfred Schutz and the Myth of Phenomenological Social Science. About 300 pp.*
Jarvie, Ian C. Concepts and Society. *216 pp.*
●**Pelz, Werner.** The Scope of Understanding in Sociology. *Towards a more radical reorientation in the social humanistic sciences. 283 pp.*
Roche, Maurice. Phenomenology, Language and the Social Sciences. *371 pp.*
Sahay, Arun. Sociological Analysis. *212 pp.*
Sklair, Leslie. The Sociology of Progress. *320 pp.*
Slater, P. Origin and Significance of the Frankfurt School. *A Marxist Perspective. About 192 pp.*
Smart, Barry. Sociology, Phenomenology and Marxian Analysis. *A Critical Discussion of the Theory and Practice of a Science of Society. 220 pp.*

International Library of Anthropology

General Editor Adam Kuper

Ahmed, A. S. Millenium and Charisma Among Pathans. *A Critical Essay in Social Anthropology. 192 pp.*
Brown, Paula. The Chimbu. *A Study of Change in the New Guinea Highlands. 151 pp.*
Gudeman, Stephen. Relationships, Residence and the Individual. *A Rural Panamanian Community. 288 pp. 11 Plates, 5 Figures, 2 Maps, 10 Tables.*
Hamnett, Ian. Chieftainship and Legitimacy. *An Anthropological Study of Executive Law in Lesotho. 163 pp.*
Hanson, F. Allan. Meaning in Culture. *127 pp.*
Lloyd, P. C. Power and Independence. *Urban Africans' Perception of Social Inequality. 264 pp.*

Pettigrew, Joyce. Robber Noblemen. *A Study of the Political System of the Sikh Jats. 284 pp.*

Street, Brian V. The Savage in Literature. *Representations of 'Primitive' Society in English Fiction, 1858–1920. 207 pp.*

Van Den Berghe, Pierre L. Power and Privilege at an African University. *278 pp.*

International Library of Social Policy

General Editor Kathleen Jones

Bayley, M. Mental Handicap and Community Care. *426 pp.*

Bottoms, A. E., and **McClean, J. D.** Defendants in the Criminal Process. *284 pp.*

Butler, J. R. Family Doctors and Public Policy. *208 pp.*

Davies, Martin. Prisoners of Society. *Attitudes and Aftercare. 204 pp.*

Gittus, Elizabeth. Flats, Families and the Under-Fives. *285 pp.*

Holman, Robert. Trading in Children. *A Study of Private Fostering. 355 pp.*

Jones, Howard, and **Cornes, Paul.** Open Prisons. *About 248 pp.*

Jones, Kathleen. History of the Mental Health Service. *428 pp.*

Jones, Kathleen, with **Brown, John, Cunningham, W. J., Roberts, Julian,** and **Williams, Peter.** Opening the Door. *A Study of New Policies for the Mentally Handicapped. 278 pp.*

Karn, Valerie. Retiring to the Seaside. *About 280 pp. 2 maps. Numerous tables.*

Thomas, J. E. The English Prison Officer since 1850: *A Study in Conflict. 258 pp.*

Walton, R. G. Women in Social Work. *303 pp.*

Woodward, J. To Do the Sick No Harm. *A Study of the British Voluntary Hospital System to 1875. 221 pp.*

International Library of Welfare and Philosophy

General Editors Noel Timms and David Watson

● **Plant, Raymond.** Community and Ideology. *104 pp.*

● **McDermott, F. E.** (Ed.) Self-Determination in Social Work. *A Collection of Essays on Self-determination and Related Concepts by Philosophers and Social Work Theorists. Contributors: F. P. Biestek, S. Bernstein, A. Keith-Lucas, D. Sayer, H. H. Perelman, C. Whittington, R. F. Stalley, F. E. McDermott, I. Berlin, H. J. McCloskey, H. L. A. Hart, J. Wilson, A. I. Melden, S. I. Benn. 254 pp.*

Ragg, Nicholas M. People Not Cases. *A Philosophical Approach to Social Work. About 250 pp.*

13

● **Timms, Noel,** and **Watson, David** (Eds). Talking About Welfare. *Readings in Philosophy and Social Policy. Contributors: T. H. Marshall, R. B. Brandt, G. H. von Wright, K. Nielsen, M. Cranston, R. M. Titmuss, R. S. Downie, E. Telfer, D. Donnison, J. Benson, P. Leonard, A. Keith-Lucas, D. Walsh, I. T. Ramsey. 320 pp.*

Primary Socialization, Language and Education

General Editor Basil Bernstein

Adlam, Diana S., *with the assistance of Geoffrey Turner and Lesley Lineker.* Code in Context. *About 272 pp.*

Bernstein, Basil. Class, Codes and Control. *3 volumes.*
    1. *Theoretical Studies Towards a Sociology of Language. 254 pp.*
    2. *Applied Studies Towards a Sociology of Language. 377 pp.*
●   3. *Towards a Theory of Educatiomal Transmission. 167 pp.*

Brandis, W., and **Bernstein, B.** Selection and Control. *176 pp.*

Brandis, Walter, and **Henderson, Dorothy.** Social Class, Language and Communication. *288 pp.*

Cook-Gumperz, Jenny. Social Control and Socialization. *A Study of Class Differences in the Language of Maternal Control. 290 pp.*

● **Gahagan, D. M.,** and **G. A.** Talk Reform. *Exploration in Language for Infant School Children. 160 pp.*

Hawkins, P. R. Social Class, the Nominal Group and Verbal Strategies. *About 220 pp.*

Robinson, W. P., and **Rackstraw, Susan D. A.** A Question of Answers. *2 volumes. 192 pp. and 180 pp.*

Turner, Geoffrey J., and **Mohan, Bernard A.** A Linguistic Description and Computer Programme for Children's Speech. *208 pp.*

Reports of the Institute of Community Studies

● **Cartwright, Ann.** Parents and Family Planning Services. *306 pp.*
    Patients and their Doctors. *A Study of General Practice. 304 pp.*

Dench, Geoff. Maltese in London. *A Case-study in the Erosion of Ethnic Consciousness. 302 pp.*

● **Jackson, Brian.** Streaming: *an Education System in Miniature. 168 pp.*

Jackson, Brian, and **Marsden, Dennis.** Education and the Working Class: *Some General Themes raised by a Study of 88 Working-class Children in a Northern Industrial City. 268 pp. 2 folders.*

Marris, Peter. The Experience of Higher Education. *232 pp. 27 tables.*
    Loss and Change. *192 pp.*

Marris, Peter, and **Rein, Martin.** Dilemmas of Social Reform. *Poverty and Community Action in the United States. 256 pp.*

Marris, Peter, and Somerset, Anthony. African Businessmen. *A Study of Entrepreneurship and Development in Kenya. 256 pp.*

Mills, Richard. Young Outsiders: *a Study in Alternative Communities. 216 pp.*

Runciman, W. G. Relative Deprivation and Social Justice. *A Study of Attitudes to Social Inequality in Twentieth-Century England. 352 pp.*

Willmott, Peter. Adolescent Boys in East London. *230 pp.*

Willmott, Peter, and Young, Michael, Family and Class in a London Suburb. *202 pp. 47 tables.*

Young, Michael. Innovation and Research in Education. *192 pp.*

●Young, Michael, and McGeeney, Patrick. Learning Begins at Home. *A Study of a Junior School and its Parents. 128 pp.*

Young, Michael, and Willmott, Peter. Family and Kinship in East London. *Foreword by Richard M. Titmuss. 252 pp. 39 tables.*
The Symmetrical Family. *410 pp.*

Reports of the Institute for Social Studies in Medical Care

Cartwright, Ann, Hockey, Lisbeth, and Anderson, John L. Life Before Death. *310 pp.*

Dunnell, Karen, and Cartwright, Ann. Medicine Takers, Prescribers and Hoarders. *190 pp.*

Medicine, Illness and Society

General Editor W. M. Williams

Robinson, David. The Process of Becoming Ill. *142 pp.*

Stacey, Margaret, *et al.* Hospitals, Children and Their Families. *The Report of a Pilot Study. 202 pp.*

Stimson, G. V., and Webb, B. Going to See the Doctor. *The Consultation Process in General Practice. 155 pp.*

Monographs in Social Theory

General Editor Arthur Brittan

●Barnes, B. Scientific Knowledge and Sociological Theory. *192 pp.*

Bauman, Zygmunt. Culture as Praxis. *204 pp.*

●Dixon, Keith. Sociological Theory. *Pretence and Possibility. 142 pp.*

Meltzer, B. N., Petras, J. W., and Reynolds, L. T. Symbolic Interactionism. *Genesis, Varieties and Criticisms. 144 pp.*

●Smith, Anthony D. The Concept of Social Change. *A Critique of the Functionalist Theory of Social Change. 208 pp.*

Routledge Social Science Journals

The British Journal of Sociology. *Editor – Angus Stewart; Associate Editor – Leslie Sklair. Vol. 1, No. 1 – March 1950 and Quarterly. Roy. 8vo. All back issues available. An international journal publishing original papers in the field of sociology and related areas.*

Community Work. *Edited by David Jones and Marjorie Mayo. 1973. Published annually.*

Economy and Society. *Vol. 1, No. 1. February 1972 and Quarterly. Metric Roy. 8vo. A journal for all social scientists covering sociology, philosophy, anthropology, economics and history. All back numbers available.*

Religion. Journal of Religion and Religions. *Chairman of Editorial Board, Ninian Smart. Vol. 1, No. 1, Spring 1971. A journal with an inter-disciplinary approach to the study of the phenomena of religion. All back numbers available.*

Year Book of Social Policy in Britain, The. *Edited by Kathleen Jones. 1971. Published annually.*

Social and Psychological Aspects of Medical Practice

Editor Trevor Silverstone

Lader, Malcolm. Psychophysiology of Mental Illness. *280 pp.*
● **Silverstone, Trevor,** and **Turner, Paul.** Drug Treatment in Psychiatry. *232 pp.*

Printed in Great Britain by Unwin Brothers Limited
The Gresham Press Old Woking Surrey
A member of the Staples Printing Group